From Pigeons
to Tweets

To Marsha
Thank you for your
support of our
wounded warriors!
God Bless!
"Mae" McKnight
Lt. Gen USA (Ret)
17 Jan 2016

From Pigeons to Tweets

The Dramatic Revolution in Military Communications

by
**Lt. Gen. Clarence E. McKnight, Jr.
(U.S. Army -Ret)**
with
Hank H. Cox

We recommend that no Hamas operatives,
whether low level or senior leaders, show their faces above
ground in the days ahead.
—Israeli Defense ForceNovember 14, 2012
(Declaring war with a tweet)

History Publishing Company
Palisades, New York

Publisher's Cataloging-in-Publication
(Provided by Quality Books, Inc.)

McKnight, Clarence E., 1929-
    From pigeons to tweets : a general who led dramatic
changes in military communications / Clarence E.
McKnight, Jr. ; with Hank H. Cox.
    p. cm.
    Includes index.
    LCCN 2012954202
    ISBN-13: 9781933909233
    ISBN-10: 1933909234
    ISBN-13: 9781933909776 (e-book)
    ISBN-10: 1933909773 (e-book)

    1. McKnight, Clarence E., 1929- 2. Generals--United
States--Biography. 3. United States. Army--Officers--
Biography. 4. Communications, Military. I. Cox, Hank
H., 1945- II. Title.

E748.M49A3 2012   973.92'092
                             QBI12-600228

Dedication

To the sergeants and warrant officers of the
Signal Corps who always find a way to get it done.

TABLE OF CONTENTS

ACKNOWLEDGMENTS

WHEN ANYONE MY AGE SETS OUT TO RELATE HIS LIFE STORY, there is always the clear and present danger of being betrayed by memory. With the passage of years, some memories tend to expand and others to disappear entirely. I would like to express my deepest appreciation to the many friends and colleagues who took time to help me assemble my memories from years past to construct this story, and to "embellish" many of them in order to bring them closer to the reality of what actually happened.

Not surprisingly, most of these people were fellow Army officers who served with me in one capacity or another over the years. Foremost among these is my dear friend Lt. Gen. Julius Becton, who generously contributed the Foreword. John Grimes, who served as Assistant Secretary of Defense in two administrations, one Republican and one Democrat, provided extensive input and took time to review the entire manuscript on my behalf. I cannot thank you enough, John. Others who took time to be interviewed include Leo Childs, Robert Donahue, Alan Salisbury, Robert Nabors and George O'Brien. Special thanks also to Professor Mike Kelly who is a pioneer in digital education, and Marie Lerch, Booz Allen Vice President for Public Relations and Marketing.

I thank you all for helping me tell this story. And if this story should prove inaccurate in any respect, it is your fault.

FOREWORD

THE SIGNAL CORPS HAS ALWAYS BEEN ONE OF THE ARMY'S foremost incubators of technological innovation, and few if any leaders in that illustrious organization have brought more vision, creative energy, or made more enduring contributions , than my good friend, Lieutenant General Clarence E. McKnight—whom I know simply as "Mac."

The last half century has seen a revolution in communications technology that has forever transformed the way in which we work, live and fight. In my lifetime, we have evolved from Morse code transmissions, rudimentary analog telephones and paper spewing teletype machines, to digital communications, globally capable cellular telephones, satellites and fiber optic enabled networks, and the Internet. Every month seems to bring a dizzying array of revolutionary technological breakthroughs that would have been unimaginable, even a few years before.

This unprecedented revolution in Information Technology (IT) posed significant challenges to all aspects of military's business and combat operations but particularly command, control, maneuver, logistics and intelligence—all of which are critically dependent upon rapid, reliable and survivable communications. The massive firepower, lightning fast maneuver, and superior training which are the hallmarks of our combat units, would count for little, were we not able to discern the movements, capabilities and intent of the enemy, and to provide real time information up and down the chain of command. In the heat of battle, the rapid and reliable transmission of secure information can spell the difference between victory and defeat. Information technology, as the key enabler of cyber warfare, has now become the fifth domain of warfare, along with ground, sea, air and space, and as such, is now a decisive military capability in its own right. Mac, over the years, was a major player in driving the Army's response to the IT and cyber revolutions.

I love the title of Mac's book, "From Pigeons to Tweets," because it really does capture the dramatic changes that have taken place in modern communications. It wasn't really so long ago that Mac, as a freshly-minted second lieutenant in the Korean War, was repairing wires along the ground between ground troops and commanders, and actually caring for carrier pigeons that-thank God-we never actually had to depend upon, at least not then. I was also a lieutenant in that conflict fighting on the front lines against a formidable, desperate, and resourceful enemy. I learned early the vital importance of real time communications on the battlefield, and the importance of dedicated and determined officers like Mac who routinely risked their lives to make certain the "voice of command" went through.

By the time I got to work with Mac directly, I was a lieutenant general commanding the VII Corps in Germany in the late 70s, and Mac was a major general commanding the 5th Signal Command-responsible for the Army's communications network throughout most of Western Europe. It was Mac's fourth tour in Germany and he had long since mastered the complexities and challenges inherent in that demanding environment. While you could more effectively use wireless communications across the open plains in the northern part of the country, down in the southern mountains, where my command was based, the rugged terrain made all forms of wireless communications more challenging. In those days, digital communications and the myriad technological advantages which it offered were still a pipedream. However, Mac, ever the visionary, learned to use the excellent German telephone network as a basis to extend our communications and overcome the formidable geographic obstacles posed by mountainous terrain. He ordered the installation of junction boxes on telephone poles throughout the region-an innovative system that saved us both time and money. All we had to do was send a technician up a local telephone pole to patch into the national commercial telephone grid in order to achieve non-secure communications throughout the region, and indeed access to the rest of the world. This basic system served us well until we developed far more advanced transmission, encryption, and voice, data and video platform technologies which would take communications to an entirely different level.

This of course was at the height of the Cold War and our primary mission was to be ready to repel a Soviet invasion of Western Europe which we assumed would mean massive, simultaneous, air and ground advances through the Fulda Gap in the north and the heart of the VII Corps in the south. A key part of our readiness strategy was the annual REFORGER (Return of Forces to Germany) Exercise in which we moved substantial military units from the United States to Germany as quickly as possible, and positioned them to do battle as they would do in case the Cold War became a "Hot War."

REFORGER, of course, presented massive logistical challenges to all phases of military operations, including communications. The complexity of the challenge was daunting in the extreme. Even then, the changing technologies of battlefield communications demanded a lot of our troops who had to adapt to an unfamiliar environment very quickly, sometimes using communications media that were not fully compatible. I learned early on that with Mac in charge, I did not have to worry about communications. He was one of those rare leaders with tremendous energy and resourcefulness who never got rattled. When problems arose, he dealt with them quickly and efficiently. Where "going by the book" was insufficient, he had a never ending bag of tricks in his duffle bag that found a way around the problem. Many years before, a senior officer had said of Mac that he could "communicate out of Hell," and I believe it was true. Mac always found a way.

Of course, in the Army no one does anything alone. We don't have solo acts. We have many thousands of specialists working through a well-established chain of command. To be effective, an officer must have the confidence of both his superiors and subordinates. Mac was second to none in his ability to work with people throughout the organization. His superiors knew they could trust and rely on him, as did his subordinates. There was never anything phony about Mac. He cared about people and it showed. The junior officers and enlisted personnel reporting to Mac were dedicated and highly motivated, a profound testimony to his leadership. Indeed, in my book, that is the one true test of real leadership.

Mac's resourcefulness and genuine concern for his troops was manifest in the often frantic run-up to military exercises and also in the routine, day-to-day activities that characterize the bulk of military life. Many things that appear simple today, and which are in fact simple today, were exceedingly tough back then. For example, Mac made sure the troops in Germany-including we higher ups-were able to watch the Super Bowl. I don't know how he did it. There was no ubiquitous, multichannel, English speaking global broadcast satellite/cable TV network available; nor an Internet streaming video capability. In those days we relied upon a fragile, single channel, weather sensitive, single thread, low power, microwave military network called the Armed Forces Radio and TV System (AFRTS). Yet, I remember routinely watching the games and listening to our troops root for their favorite teams, just like they would have been doing back home-so Mac somehow "got it done".

Mac assumed responsibility for the modernization of the European Telephone System (ETS), replacing obsolete mechanical switching equipment and pre-World War II designed "cord board" operator assistance capability with state of the art technology. There were naturally a great many glitches as the older system was replaced with the newer one, but Mac took the heat and got it done with minimal disruptions.

Mac also played the lead role in modernizing communications to facilitate more effective command and control of the U.S. tactical nuclear arsenal in Europe. This was obviously a delicate and challenging responsibility with intense oversight from both the collective political and military leadership of the United States and NATO. Mac supervised the replacement of an obsolete system, the European Command and Control Console System (ECCCS), with a state-of-the-art redundant system built on two mobile capabilities. The first employed satellite technology, the Flaming Arrow Net employing the AN/MSC 64 UHF satellite terminal, and the other, a high frequency radio system called Regency Net. He got rid of the old ECCCS with its fixed microwave transmitters mounted on huge, static, orange and white steel towers that would have been destroyed immediately as the precursor to a conventional war. But no transition of this scale and complexity is ever managed smoothly or without conflict. It was part of Mac's genius that he guided the process to completion with a minimum of confusion and controversy.

One of our command decisions while Mac and I served together was to consolidate the myriad scattered Signal Battalions located in southern Germany into a centralized Signal Brigade, a shift that enabled communications from the theater Army commander down to the lowest combat echelon, and also significant gains in efficiency, effectiveness and cost control.

Mac told me we were free to assign any number to that Brigade, and he suggested we call it the 93rd Signal Brigade. As it happened, when I first served in the Army in World War II, I was assigned to the 93rd Division, an all-black unit, in the Pacific. Mac scored more than a few points with me on that one.

I have heard it said that Mac describes me as a mentor. I am proud to accept that accolade with the understanding that both he and I had many mentors during our military careers. As I said, you don't go anything alone in the Army. I may have mentored him and many other fine officers throughout their careers. Mac did likewise, and it was widely noted that many of the younger officers whom he subsequently helped achieve star rank were minorities like myself. The U.S. military is a "meritocracy" that really does live and breathe equal opportunity. This is true in large measure to the tireless efforts of fine men like Mac McKnight who didn't just "talk the talk" but also courageously "walked the walk". At my request, Mac even made the Black History Month speech at the Memorial Chapel, Ft Myer where we both attended the Sunday service.

However, I think that Mac's most lasting contribution to posterity will not be measured in his considerable achievements in the Army; but rather in his continuing dedication to helping our nation's young people adapt to changing technologies and prepare for productive lives in the future. He was instrumental in creating the National Science Center, now being moved from Augusta, Georgia, to Washington, D.C., where thousands of youngsters have experienced firsthand, advanced science, technology, engineering and mathematics. Mac was also one of the driving forces behind launching the Community Learning and Information Network (CLIN), an interactive online educational system that became the prototype of the Distributed Training Technology Project (DTTP), used by Reserve units and National Guards to provide interactive training directly to local communities. The DTTP was the first broadband network in the country.

Mac is also in the forefront of the national campaign for educational reform and is spearheading an effort to promote an educational model that offers great promise of a future public school system in which online technologies greatly enhance the learning process, empower teachers and command the attention of more of our young people.

In the final analysis, Mac's autobiography is a story of service-to his country, his family, his faith and the future. He continues to serve and with God's grace will continue for a long time. He is one of the best. I am grateful that I was privileged to serve with him, grateful for his friendship and especially grateful for his example.

Lt. Gen. Julius Becton, Jr.
U.S. Army-ret

CHAPTER ONE

Career Choices

I shall be telling this with a sigh
Somewhere ages and ages hence;
Two roads diverged in a wood, and I—
I took the one less traveled by,
And that has made all the difference.
                              —Robert Frost

ROBERT E. LEE GRADUATED NEAR THE TOP OF HIS CLASS AT West Point. By doing so well, he was able to choose which branch of the service he wanted to serve in. And like just about every West Point grad before and since who had that choice, he chose the Corps of Engineers. Then as now, it was seen by professional military officers as the most promising route to achieving higher rank. Also you get to build things.

I served all of my military career in the Signal Corps, and it was to prove a most advantageous career choice. Over my lifetime, the work of the Signal Corps has coincided with a revolution in communications technology, posing formidable challenges to both military and civilian communications, and commensurate opportunity to those who could manage the transition. I did very well in this environment as my three stars will attest. But in truth, I had no notion when I entered West Point of going with the Signal Corps. My first choice was always the Corps of Engineers. Unfortunately, I graduated about mid-pack of the Class of '52 (206 out of 528), and about 50 or more of my classmates were ahead of me on the list of applicants for the Corps of Engineers.[1]

That was a major disappointment to me. It wasn't just a matter of the promise of career advancement, though I, like most young officers, was certainly ambitious for advancement. But I had always wanted to be a civil engineer, which was the main reason I set my sights on the academy. But though I was a pretty good student at my high school in Memphis, Tennessee, where I was graduated as salutatorian, I had been unable to wrangle an appointment to West Point, at least not at first. I ended up at the University of Tennessee in Knoxville on a part time basis, mainly because my family had limited financial means. I worked to earn money and took as many classes as I could, mostly in engineering.

I wasn't at UT long, but my brief sojourn there was interesting. I ran for vice president of the freshman class and lost, but I attracted the notice of an up and coming upper classman named Howard Baker, the same Howard Baker who would later have a long and distinguished career in the U.S. Senate. In those days, the big fraternities pretty much ran the campus, but Baker had a plan to change the power structure. He had noticed me in my unsuccessful run for a freshman office and liked what he saw. He asked me to join his ticket and run for president of the sophomore class while he ran for president of the senior class. Somehow we persuaded a beauty queen named Sugar Smith, who was Miss Tennessee, to participate in our campaign. I remember the three of us went tooling down the boulevards in Knoxville with a loud speaker playing a song entitled, "My Sugar

---

[1] My good friend and colleague of many years Alan Salisbury, Major General U.S. Army (Ret), tells me that today West Point graduates list infantry and armor as their top choices, not the Corps of Engineers. He said they are also less focused on becoming general officers. Rather, they want to lead troops in combat.

Is So Refined." We swept the election, which in retrospect doesn't seem all that remarkable given the presence of Howard Baker at the top of the ticket.

Still I had high hopes of getting into West Point, which of course is a free education and one of the best engineering schools in the country. I had taken the entrance examination, had earned a ranking as a third alternate, and was granted an interview by another Tennessean, Carl Hubb Hinkle, a former Air Force General in World War II who had been knocked back to a permanent rank of Lieutenant Colonel after the war. He was serving as a tactical officer at West Point. Hinkle asked me why I thought I was a good candidate for West Point. I told him I was a leader. He asked me, what makes you think you're a leader? I said because I got elected president of the sophomore class at UT. He thought that was uproariously funny.

For reasons still unclear to me, shortly after that election I was in fact invited to West Point. I presume the candidates ahead of me dropped out for some reason, and maybe Hinkle put in a good word for me too. But I should add that I really did have a few other things to commend me besides being president of the sophomore class at UT. For example, I was a member in good standing of the Key Club, the junior Kiwanis Club, which has a nationwide network. They put me up for Lieutenant Governor of the Key Club in West Tennessee and Northern Arkansas. I won and got to do some traveling for them. In any case, I received that coveted West Point appointment and was thrilled to get it. I was on my way to becoming an engineer.

I was in for a rude awakening. I had been having a good old time at UT. Many if not most of my classmates were WWII veterans going to college on the GI bill. The head of my fraternity was a 32-year old former bomber pilot. I was in ROTC and hit it off with the vets. They let me use their textbooks, saving me money. I probably would have been able to complete my education there eventually, had I not got the call to become one of the Black Knights of the Hudson.

But West Point was not at all like UT. It was rigorous regimentation from the moment you got out of bed until you went back to bed, and there were a lot of hours in between. The curriculum was daunting to say the least. And of course the first year students like me, the plebes, caught a truckload of hazing and petty criticism. I have never cared to be pushed around and force-fed nonsense, but that is a traditional part of the first year program at all of the military academies.

I will never forget we all had to travel to Washington, D.C., in 1949 to march in President Truman's inaugural parade. That meant I had to stay at West Point over the Christmas holidays, which was something of a disappointment. Like most people, I prefer to spend Christmas with my family. I remember it was very cold that day and we had to march nine miles. I don't think Washington is actually more than nine miles wide at any given point, but somehow they had us marching nine miles in that parade. Man, it was some kind of cold.

At some point that first year, when I was feeling especially down in spirit, I called my mother in Memphis and told her I had made a big mistake, and that West Point was just not for me. She brought me up short. She said I was getting a free education and she and my father had dug deep in their pockets to pay my fare up there. She urged me to hang in for at least the first year.

This led to some serious soul-searching. I thought the world of my mother. She was a very religious woman and totally committed to me and my older sister. She was not stern, but there was always something about her that made me determined to earn her approval, or at least not disappoint her. So I resolved to stick it out that first year and along the way I began to get some encouragement from the upper classmen. So I made it through the Long Gray Line—and, lucky me, I soon found myself running communications wires along the ground in Korea while a variety of hostile people lobbed artillery shells in my direction. Who could ask for more?

The Signal Corps

I cannot recall at this late date whether I applied for the Signal Corps or they reached out to me, but in either case it was clear they wanted me. By that time, I was of course fully aware of how important the Signal Corps was to the military. You pick up a lot of that kind of information at West Point. For example, more than a few historians believe that Robert E. Lee and the rebel army lost the Battle of Gettysburg, and possibly the Civil War, because his senior cavalry commander J.E.B. Stuart was off capturing a Union supply caravan when he should have been scouting the Army of the Potomac for his commander. Lee was left groping in the dark wondering where General George Meade was placing his divisions. By the time Lee figured it out, it was too late. Some senior Confederate officers thought Stuart should have been court martialed for that, but Lee demurred. (On the other hand, I shudder to think of what would have happened to our country if the rebels had prevailed.)

Then and now, in every military strategy and on every battlefield, information is critical to the outcome. Commanders need to know what the enemy is up to and capable of. They need to know where their forces are and where to direct artillery and air strikes. Lack of information and, even worse, incorrect information, can and will lead to defeat. During WWII our victory in the pivotal Battle of Midway was made possible in large measure because we had partially broken the Japanese code and were reasonably certain where they were and what they were doing. At the same time, we could communicate with our own forces securely. Much of the credit for our superiority in this regard belongs with the Signal Corps.

The Signal Corps was founded by Albert J. Myer, after

whom Fort Myer in Arlington, Virginia, is named. Myer trained as a physician and later worked as a telegraph operator. Myer wrote his medical dissertation on "A New Sign Language for Deaf Mutes" which may have been his inspiration for a military visual communications system. He joined the Army as a surgeon and by 1856 was pitching a new battlefield signaling system using semaphore flags he had developed that he called "wigwag" to Secretary of War Jefferson Davis, who would later serve as President of the Confederacy. Davis put him off, but Myer was undeterred.

Myer had a natural instinct for working with politicians—a quality I admire—and by 1860 he had worked himself into a military appropriations bill as a signal officer with the rank of major. When the Civil War broke out, Myer ended up in Fort Monroe, Virginia, providing signaling for the Army of the Potomac and training a new corps of signal officers and men. He launched a campaign to create an independent Signal Corps and in March 1863, President Abraham Lincoln signed legislation translating Myer's vision into reality. Thus, the Signal Corps came into existence and Myer became the first Chief Signal Officer as a Colonel.

Communications during that period were primitive by todays' standards. They had the telegraph of course and spent much of the Civil War stringing wire for the telegraph along the routes followed by military units. They sent men up in hot air balloons to survey enemy dispositions. But Myer's main technical contribution was probably the "wigwag" system using semaphore flags to send instructions to combat units in action. The Union army created signal stations at various high points along the line, reporting where the Confederate army was concentrating its strength. General Meade used signal flags to move his troops where they were needed at Gettysburg, enabling him to win that great victory. (The Confederates, by the way, had their own signaling system, created by officers who had worked with Myer.)

By World War I, the Signal Corps was using airplanes to perform reconnaissance of enemy positions, but the military role superseded the intelligence gathering function in the air, and in 1917 General John J. Pershing separated the air wing from the Signal Corps. Pershing divided the Land Section of the Corps into four groups: combat photography, pigeons, meteorology and radio intelligence. The Corps was using radio technology increasingly to communicate with front line troops. Although photography had been a Corps responsibility since 1881, Pershing's order made it an official mission. Field photography consisted of ground and aerial, and ground photography included motion pictures, a first. Following the war, all aerial photography and ground photography related to aviation was transferred to the new Air Corps.

The Pigeon Service's primary mission was to create and maintain a frontline communications system based on birds. In November 1917, two detachments of "pigeoneers" were in France. Pigeon communications were employed in several engagements, including the St. Mihiel and Meuse-Argonne offensives. One particular pigeon named Cher Ami won a Distinguished Service Cross by delivering a message about the location of the celebrated "Lost Battalion." Pigeons successfully delivered 95 percent of its messages assigned to them. After the war, the Pigeon Service was officially demobilized, but the Signal Corps still had some around until 1957.

During that war the Signal Corps had set up a research and development operation in Washington, D.C. In 1918, that operation was transferred to a facility in New Jersey that would later become Fort Monmouth, and the major hub of Signal Corp R&D and operations.

During World War II, when the U.S. was totally mobilized

and engaged in combat operations all over the globe, the Signal Corps truly came into its own. We were providing a wide range of communications expertise, from management of radar stations to battlefield communications to production of propaganda films. By mid-1942, a few months into the war, the Corps claimed 7,694 officers, 121,727 enlisted men and 54,000 civilians. By mid-1943, when mobilization was virtually complete, and the Army had reached its authorized strength of 7.7 million men, the Corps had 27,000 officers and 287,000 enlisted men. A growing number of Signal Corp personnel were women and minorities at a time when strict racial segregation was still the norm in most parts of military and civilian life, a fact of which I am proud.

During WWII, the Signal Corps had its nose in just about every aspect of communications and intelligence gathering, except perhaps undercover espionage. While safeguarding the Army's own communications, the Corps attempted to breach the security of enemy signals. In the field, radio intelligence units located enemy stations and intercepted them. We broke the Japanese codes and helped the British crack the German codes. The Corps also played an active role in the radio deception that preceded the allied invasion of Normandy in 1944.

Radios came into widespread use on the battlefield for the first time. The armored forces adopted FM radios in the 500 series and those in the 600 series belonged to the Field Artillery. The clarity of the static-free FM signals allowed soldiers to communicate over the noise of artillery and tank firing. One infantry battalion radio operator wrote: "FM saved lives and won battles because it speeded our communications and enabled us to move more quickly than the Germans, who had to depend on AM."[2]

---

[2]Taken from "Getting the Message Through," by Rebecca Robbins Raines, published by Center of Military History, United States Army, 1996. Though I was an active player in the evolution of the Signal Corps during this period, I am grateful to Rebecca and her excellent book for much of the information reported here.

But we began to encounter even then a problem that continues to vex battlefield communications to this day-evolving technologies that are often incompatible. During WWII, we made great progress in improving communications capabilities, but they were not always synchronized. The FM walkie-talkie could not communicate with the AM handie-talkie. Moreover, because the frequency range of FM tank radios did not overlap that of the walkie-talkie, tank-infantry teams could not talk to each other. Various attempts were made to reconcile the two systems, but the war ended without a satisfactory solution.

Many years later, I found myself in a heated exchange with a senior general who wanted to forego spending on radios so he could use the money to build more tanks. I explained to him that the German Panzers in WWII were effective because they had radios and could communicate with each other. "Without communications, a tank is just a hunk of steel," I told him. I won that argument.

The end of WWII brought a sharp reduction in Signal Corps forces, as it did for all military operations. By June 1946, the Corps strength had dwindled to only 56,000 officers and men, scarcely one sixth of its wartime composition. Many of its field agencies and training facilities were shut down. The Corps also lost many functions to the Air Force and the Army Security Agency. Most Signal Corps functions were consolidated at Fort Monmouth. Later the Corps added a training center at Fort Gordon, Georgia, which I in later years would command, (and where I received my third star).

But that was way off in the future. In June 1950, North Korean forces invaded South Korea, which would provide my baptism of fire when I was graduated from West Point two years later. The Signal Corps, like many military arms, was unprepared for the Korean conflict. There was a shortage of signal units to take the field. Those that went had to "cannibalize" units left behind for the equipment they needed, much of which was left over from WWII.

Poor communications were a factor in our military's early reverses in Korea. It took a long time to establish wire-based communications because of the rough topography. In some cases, the Corps actually used airplanes to lay communications wire across rough terrain. Early on, the troops were depending on very high frequency (VHF), or microwave, radios until we could get wires laid. The VHF radios depended on line-of-sight transmission. The aging batteries died quickly and replacements were hard to come by. The bitter climate also took a toll on the batteries. In that environment, it is not surprising that someone sent carrier pigeons from Fort Monmouth to Korea, but we really never had to put them to serious use. The pigeon program was finally phased out in 1957.

Our equipment was poor, but the North Koreans were even worse off, using old WWII stuff supplied by the Soviet Union. Much of the time they were communicating with whistles, bugles and horns. That was probably what the ancient Romans used. By the time the Korean conflict sputtered out, the U.S. Army had suffered nearly 110,000 casualties, 334 of them from the Signal Corps.

By the end of 1953, the Signal Corps had grown to 7,500 officers and 83,000 enlisted men. Those ranks began to diminish rapidly when the Korean conflict ended, of course, but it left behind a growing awareness that increasingly sophisticated communication devices were changing the nature of battlefield communications. Thus, that conflict stimulated long-term expansion of the Corps' research and development program. At a new specially designed facility known as the Hexagon at Fort Monmouth, called the U.S. Army Signal Research and Development Laboratory, the Corps began working seriously on miniaturization and systems integration.

We were making progress. Using newly-developed vacuum tubes, we came up with a smaller handie-talkie that operated on FM and was finally compatible with the walkie-talkie. The Corps also came up with a new generation of FM vehicular radios whose components could be easily replaced, and also worked with the handie-talkie and the walkie-talkie. A new portable typewriter weighed only 45 pounds, one-fifth as much as the older equipment, and could be carried by a paratrooper on a drop. It was waterproof and could transmit messages more than twice as fast as previous models. Field switchboards weighing just 22 pounds appeared and field telephones also were slimmed down.

The advent of transistors obviously made possible further breakthroughs in communications devices and the subsequent invention in 1958 of the integrated circuit, or electronic microchip, made possible tremendous strides in miniaturization. But the intense experimentation at Fort Monmouth on electronic warfare became a liability because of interference from neighboring radio and TV stations, airports and other electronic signals. Consequently, in 1954 the Army set up the Electronic Proving Ground at Fort Huachuca (pronounced wa-chukka) in an isolated spot in Arizona about 70 miles south of Tucson. That fort, another future command for yours truly, had been the site of a heliograph station during the campaign against Geronimo in the 1880s. Work there over the years involved battlefield surveillance, avionics and meteorology.

In 1957, the Corps established the U.S. Army Combat Surveillance Agency to carry out its missions of combat surveillance and target acquisition. The agency also coordinated the Corps' efforts with those of other agencies working on drone aircraft, ground and airborne radar and infrared sensors.

Under the 1947 defense act, the Army got responsibility for tactical missiles while the Air Force handled strategic weapons.

The Army conducted its guided missile research at the White Sands Proving Ground in New Mexico, yet another future posting for me. Werner Von Braun, the German rocket scientist we acquired after WWII, had led a team of experts there before they moved on to the Redstone Arsenal in Alabama. Meanwhile, the Signal Corps set up a field agency at White Sands to provide missile range instrumentation. Among other things, we developed the Missile Master, an electronic fire control system for Nike air defense missiles.

The Army's increased use of aviation called for a type of expanded communications support which became known as avionics-including radio communications, electronic aids to navigation, instrumentation, stabilization and aircraft identification and recognition. Lightweight equipment developed by the Signal Corps met the stringent weight requirements of the Army's relatively small aircraft. The Signal Corps became responsible for the Army Flight Information Program to furnish Army aviators with current flight data.

In my work at Huachuca and White Sands, I became deeply involved with the Corps' meteorological research and development. We had long been aware that weather impacts even the most sophisticated communications systems, causing distortions and disruptions. In 1957, the U.S. Army Signal Corps Meteorological Company, the only unit of its kind, was formed at Fort Huachuca. We ended up with nine teams scattered around the globe conducting tests, basically trying to figure out which way the wind blows. We spent a lot of money and accumulated a lot of data, but our ability to predict the weather remains about the same as those folks on the local TV stations, which is to say we're not very good at it. Only God knows what the weather is going to be and sometimes I'm not sure he knows.

The advent of the Cold War, when the nuclear threat was the primary concern of our political leaders, brought about many changes in the Signal Corps. The Army placed greater reliance on nuclear deterrence than ground forces, so troop levels declined. Leaner divisions were designed to engage on a fragmented nuclear battlefield. But such conditions placed ever greater demands on communications, and so signal companies were expanded into battalions. The Signal Corps devised an area communications system to provide invulnerability to attack, increased capacity, faster service and greater range—all predicated on the assumption of a nuclear attack. Advances in communications technology enabled us to achieve much of this, and may eventually pave the way for greater efficiency and effectiveness if we can ever learn how to manage all of the information we're generating.

A series of military reforms in the 1960s reduced the stature of the Signal Corps within the military power grid. We even lost control of Fort Monmouth which became the headquarters of the Electronics Command, an element of the Army Material Command. And as of 1964, the Office of the Chief Signal Officer was superseded by the Chief of Electronics-Communications, a subordinate agency of the Office of the Deputy Chief of Staff for Military Operations. I would not expect anyone outside the military to make heads or tails of this, but I believed then and now it was a major mistake.

Scatter Communications

The Signal Corps may have lost some clout in the various reorganizations, but it kept its responsibilities. As we wandered into the Vietnam quagmire, communications between the U.S. and Vietnam were extremely vulnerable. A single under-sea cable linked the Pacific Command in Hawaii with Guam, but it did not extend to Southeast Asia. The Army depended on high frequency radio, a medium easily jammed. To address this problem, we came up with what we call "scatter communications," by which we bounced high-frequency radio beams off layers of the atmosphere, which reflected them back to earth. One type of this, called "tropospheric scatter," bounced signals off water vapor in the troposphere, the lowest atmospheric layer. Another method, "ionospheric scatter," bounded signals off clouds of ionized particles in the ionosphere, which begins about 30 miles above the earth's surface.

The new systems offered several advantages. They provided high-quality signals less susceptible to jamming than ordinary radio, and did not require line-of-sight between stations. Tropospheric relay stations could be as far as 400 miles apart compared to 40 miles for microwave stations.

The Signal Corps was responsible for this system and encountered an array of problems that for various reasons the contractor that developed it was not responsible. For example, the harsh environment of Southeast Asia took a toll on the equipment and the system had no built in redundancy. I am a strong believer in redundancy for everything on a battlefield, especially communications. By 1965, the network began to experience severe fading of its signals. The cause was traced to a temperature inversion which occurs when the upper layers of the atmosphere are uncharacteristically warmer than lower layers.

Likewise, Signal Corps doctrine had not anticipated a fight like we had in Vietnam. It was predicated on the assumption of a nuclear war. But in Vietnam, we needed to provide fixed base communications with large antennas and heavy equipment. Divisional signal battalions had to cover operating areas of 3,000 to 5,000 square miles, compared to 200-300 in a conventional war. So signal units were scrambling for assets and trying to train personnel on the fly.

Perhaps worst of all, the system was being run by a cadre of young, inexperienced soldiers. The signal schools could not initially produce qualified graduates fast enough. The Army couldn't even track down former personnel with the appropriate skills. Throughout my military career, I have raised hell about inadequate education and training of key personnel, and nowhere was that defect more conspicuous than in the early days of the Vietnam conflict. And I cannot resist pointing out that the absence of a Chief Signal Officer, because of the earlier reorganization, left the Corps too far down in the power grid to deal effectively with its problems.

As is typical of military operations, despite great progress in technology, many signal units were stuck with WWII era equipment that would not interact with modern digital devices. When radios went out, which was often, units relied on colored smoke signals to direct artillery or call in air strikes. I believe this technology was employed by Native Americans in their futile struggle against invading Europeans. Sometimes in desperation our people in the field sent messengers, as in earlier wars, but that was a risky proposition for both the message and the messenger. At one point, they even tried to use carrier pigeons, I have no idea where they got them, Fort Monmouth was out of the pigeon business, but in any case that did not work out very well.

Our troops encountered another new phenomenon that is becoming even more challenging in our own time. There were not enough frequencies to carry the communications traffic. In 1965, a division had 15 frequencies dedicated to use of each of its three brigades. By 1967, there were only three available. The remaining 200 frequencies had to be shared with other units.

Modern readers may wonder where the satellite technology was during all this. The answer is—it was in its infancy. The Army placed an experimental satellite (SYNCOM) ground terminal in Southeast Asia in 1964 which provided a link to Hawaii, with one telephone and one teletype circuit. It was the first ever use of satellite technology in a combat zone and it was obviously quite limited.

When the Signal Corps was instructed to upgrade the telephone system throughout South Vietnam, it had only one cable construction battalion, the 40th Signal Battalion, on its rolls. Beginning in the fall of 1966, this unit installed millions of feet of cable enabling the Corps for the first time to provide dial telephone service throughout a combat zone.

The Corps continued its pictorial mission, which has always been a key part of our work since the development of modern photography. The Southeast Aria Photographic Center at Long Binh, operated by the 221st Signal Company, became the most extensive photographic facility ever operated in a combat zone.

Eventually, we established the Integrated Wideband Communications System (IWCS) which was a huge undertaking. We had to put these huge antennas up in high places. Some hilltop locations were so remote that men and equipment had to be brought in by helicopter. Bad weather and combat hindered progress. The entire IWCS comprising 67 links in South Vietnam and 33 in Thailand, totaling 470,000 circuit miles, completed in 1969, enabled commanders to control U.S. airpower throughout the region and to manage widely separated fire bases.

It was all quite impressive, but despite that investment and the sacrifice of more than 58,000 American lives, and only God knows how many Vietnamese lives, we lost the war. The moral, to me at least, is that the most advanced technologies and dedicated soldiers cannot compensate for muddled political leadership.

Unified Command

In recent years, automation and communications have become increasingly interdependent and appear to be on the verge of becoming indistinguishable. By 1978, the former chief of communications-electronics had become the assistant chief of staff for automation and communications. In 1983, the Army undertook a major realignment in the way it manages information resources. It combined five information-related functions or disciplines (communications, automation, visual information, publications/printing, and records management) into the Information Mission Area (IMA). Thus, the Army Communications Command became the Army Information Systems Command in 1984, incorporating the Army Computer Systems Command and several other elements, in order to centralize communications and the IMA under one umbrella. It was headquartered at one of my favorite places, Fort Huachuca.

It fell to me, toward the end of my career, to make this transition happen.

CHAPTER 2

A Revolution in Communications

Technology is so much fun, but we can drown in our own technology. The fog of information can drive out knowledge.
—Daniel J. Boorstin, Historian

I LAUNCHED MY MILITARY CAREER INTO THE SIGNAL CORPS in 1952, not because I foresaw the looming revolution in communications technology, but as I said before, because the Corps of Engineers wouldn't have me. In retrospect, it was a brilliant career move. Over the 35 years I served in the U.S. Army Signal Corps, and the quarter century or so that has transpired since, I have been privileged to be part of a revolution in communications technology—the digital revolution that is still transforming the way we live, work and learn. Predictably, this ongoing sea change in communications technology has had, and continues to have, a tremendous impact on military communications where the rapid transmission of accurate, secure information is often a matter of life and death, and can mean the difference between victory and defeat.

Since time immemorial, successful military leaders have understood the critical importance of timely, accurate information for situational awareness and command and control execution. The best commanders diligently sought intelligence and built that quest into their command structures. They understood also the critical importance of conveying clear instructions up and down and across echelons, especially in combat operations in the fog of war when it is most difficult to do. The Duke of Wellington sat on his horse amid the chaos of Waterloo observing the action taking place and writing lucid messages to his commanders so clear they could not be misunderstood. It was an ability shared by General Ulysses Grant in our own Civil War. Their means of communication were primitive by today's standards, pencil and paper mostly, but they fully grasped the importance of clear, concise communications. Ambiguity fosters uncertainty that can lead to catastrophe. That part of the communications challenge has not changed, and in fact has grown more daunting in a time when the sheer volume of information being conveyed often defies our ability to use it effectively. Amid the torrent of raw data dumped daily on our political, diplomatic and military leaders, there is a crying need for someone to distill it into simple, clear language that can be understood, put into perspective and acted upon.

This was a fundamental dilemma presented by the advent of automated data processing and computers. We gather mountains of data from which, after tremendous exertion, we are able to distill a few precious nuggets of knowledge, from which, after even more exertion, we may perhaps, if we are diligent and focused, glean a few precious droplets of wisdom. Today's powerful algorithms, super computer processing power and wideband networks provide real time critical situational awareness to the commander anywhere on the globe.

But that wisdom is hidden deep in the pile and will not yield itself easily or quickly. It has always been thus, but never before has the volume of raw data been so awesome and intimidating. It is a fair question whether our ability to generate all of this data, and our commensurate difficulty learning to manage it effectively, constitutes a step forward or backward. I have spent my adult life wrestling with this conundrum and, while I have no simple answer, believe I can provide some guidance to those that follow me in this continuing adventure into the unknown.

Carrier Pigeons

When I went to war in Korea in 1953 as a freshly-minted Second Lieutenant in the Signal Corps, it was my job to keep commanders in direct contact with their subordinates on the firing lines. They needed to receive timely reports of what was going on and to convey instructions in return. Our technology was primitive by today's standards and the topography of Korea posed unique challenges. We relied mainly on wires running along the ground, but these were obviously vulnerable to sabotage or breaks caused by enemy artillery fire. We had wireless radios, but the signals were sporadic and would not work well over uneven terrain. We sent written communications back and forth via small aircraft, but that was slow and not always certain. We even had some carrier pigeons "just in case" everything else failed. We never used them in actual combat, but we tested them a time or two to make sure they knew which way to fly. A signal officer in combat always assumes the worst and keeps as many backup plans in his pocket as he can. In a pinch, I am sure some of those pigeons would have gotten through.

We were even then on the cutting edge of dramatic changes to come in communications technology, but scrambling around in the Korean mud amid artillery barrages, I did not fully realize it or grasp its implications at the time. In Korea and for years later, we were mostly dependent on telephone technology provided by one unified system in our country—Ma Bell. The Signal Corps had a close working relationship with the Bell system because we were ever and always committed to innovation, and that is where the most advanced knowledge of communications technology was back then. When wars broke out, as in WWII and Korea, the Signal Corps would draft thousands of Bell employees into military service for the duration. The Signal Corps has always been a wellspring of innovation and we depended on Bell Laboratories for much of our research and development. We worked closely with them. It was one stop shopping and it worked pretty well until the breakup of the Bell system in the 1980s.

By the mid-1950s, the teletype (machine) was the primary communication medium for data. The teletype systems used Morse code straight out of the old Western Union system—which also was still around into the 1960s. People sent each other telegrams in those days. Today, that seems like something out of an old western movie. I cannot resist adding that way back in those ancient times, we would frequently communicate with each other by writing a message called a letter. You wrote or typed your message on a piece of paper, put it in an envelope, put a stamp on it and dropped it into the nearest mail box. Within a day or two, maybe longer for overseas, your letter would reach its intended recipient. There was something about getting a letter in the mail that carried more significance than an e-mail, or maybe that's just my nostalgia talking. In any case, in those days when I was off serving my country in foreign lands, I wrote letters-hundreds of letters-to my darling wife Barbara and our daughters Lynn and Marsha. They kept them and reread them, as I kept and reread their letters to me. In war and peace, in both the military and civilian worlds, communication is the very essence of our daily lives.

When the facsimile (fax) machine communication technology first came online in the mid-1960s, it became a status symbol. If you had a fax machine on your desk, whether you were in the military or private sector, it meant you were somebody. But fax machines were soon superseded by more efficient means. Fax machines still have their uses, but have given way to more advanced communications technologies.

Most electronic communications up until the 1950s and into the 1960s were conveyed on copper wires, but gradually we adopted coaxial cable and then moved on to fiber optic cables that are more reliable and can carry much more volume. Today the ocean floors are crisscrossed with communications cables. As I write we are shifting from electrical impulses to optical systems that can function even more quickly and reliably. Everything in communications is constantly getting faster.

But the cables, be they copper, coaxial or fiber optic, don't go everywhere. In the 1960s, there were only a few undersea cables connecting the major population centers of the world. When we became engaged militarily in Vietnam, the nearest cable reached the Philippines, a long way as the crow flies from Vietnam. The Signal Corps, working with Bell Labs and other private firms and research agencies, came up with what we called tropospheric and ionospheric scatter by which we bounced electronic waves off the troposphere and ionosphere.

I found myself in the Vietnamese jungle sweating with the troops using every trick in our book to enable commanders and advisors at the fire bases to communicate with the deployed soldiers. It was often a hit and miss effort. The Vietnam jungles were like a lot of places the U.S. Army found itself over the years with no established landline telephone system to hook into.

Prior to Vietnam, I was in El Salvador and Panama where the local phone systems were primitive to nonexistent. I would often employ ham radio operators to make contact with someone in the states, and then ask that person to patch us into the stateside telephone system. I was forever finding creative ways to do things. The Signal Corps has never been a safe haven for people who operate "by the book" or are easily discouraged. You don't go back to your commander and say you could not get the message through because there was six feet of snow on the ground. Your commander doesn't need a weather report, dammit, he needs you to find a way to get the communications through.

The revolution in communications technology took many forms, not the least of which was in commercial applications. In the 1950s, televisions were becoming ubiquitous in the U.S. For the first time, ordinary people could sit in their living rooms and watch live programming. It was a real breakthrough, like having a movie theater in your own house. Most of the early TVs were in black and white, but by the end of the decade, color sets were becoming common. In the early days, there were three major networks—CBS, NBC and ABC. (Public television was in its infancy then.) Every weekday evening, each network aired a national news broadcast. That was pretty much the full choice option. Those three networks had an awesome power to influence public opinion. One of the most famous and respected TV journalists was the CBS anchorman Walter Cronkite. It was reliably reported that when Cronkite came out against the Vietnam War, President Lyndon Johnson knew the game was up. He said if he had lost Cronkite, he had lost the American people, and he was probably right.

Basic television technology reigned supreme up until the early 1980s when cable networks came along. Today of course almost every American has access to cable systems that offer hundreds of channels to choose from. Such is progress, but at the same time something important was being lost. When there were only three major networks available, they were a unifying force for society. If you saw it on TV the night before, chances were good your neighbors saw it also. You had a common point of reference with other people. Today, our sources of news and entertainment are diffused over a wide range. Those other people sitting near you on the Metro or driving beside you on the highway may or may not share your insights and opinions because they are not getting the same information that you are.

Another negative about the proliferation of cable, in my humble opinion, is its deadly impact on public debate. In the old days, with only a few news outlets, we were all constantly exposed to views and ideas that challenged our own. It is a fact of life that we do not learn from people who agree with us; we learn from people who challenge us. But today when you want political commentary, you quite naturally click on the outlets that reflect your particular point of view. It makes you feel better, but you don't really learn anything. I believe this contributes to the polarization of politics in our country, making the middle ground almost uninhabitable. The problem is-democracy works most effectively when we are able to find common ground.

TV cable of course is still built upon wires of some kind—fiber optic usually—that run along telephone poles or underground. But now satellites spinning over our heads offer a whole new way of transmitting electronic signals that do not require anything on the ground except receivers. The Signal Corps put up its first communications satellite during the Vietnam War, but it was primitive by today's standards and had limited application. Today, the skies are filled to overflowing with satellites that are literally in danger of running into each other. And the air is filled with all manner of messages being sent to and fro with unheard of speed and remarkable reliability. Not all of these messages are worthy of being sent, and many should not be sent, but it is what it is.

Satellite technology greatly expanded the reach of television news. Today TV cameras are everywhere covering everything 24 hours a day and the impact on our daily lives has been profound. Who among us can keep up with it? Who even tries? No one, really. After a while, it becomes like background noise in an elevator. (And, I might add, a growing number of elevators have the endless news feeds piped in. There is no escape from it.)

Not so long ago, life moved at a more leisurely pace. Up until the Vietnam era, events around the world would be reported to the White House where our leaders would have days to sort it out, confirm it, analyze it, and respond to it before sharing it with the public. Today, news of world events is almost instantaneous for both the White House and the public at large. CNN is on the spot wherever it is, as are other international news agencies, reporting live from the earthquake or the war zone, wherever newsworthy events are happening. Our leaders are being asked to comment on events on the fly as they take place, without time to weigh, analyze and consult, often with calamitous results. Advanced communications technology has changed the whole dynamic of decision making and policy development, not necessarily for the better.

Along with revolutionary strides in communications technology came advances in computers. When I was posted to the Army missile range in White Sands, New Mexico, in 1961-62, I was put in charge of one of the first asynchronous computers, the Philco 2000, that took up an entire room. I was amazed at what that thing could do, performing hundreds of unrelated calculations simultaneously. That was the age of transistors. We quickly went through the analog era and are now into digital technology. Today, any kid in elementary school has more computing power in his backpack than we had with that Philco 2000, and just about everyone in advanced nations has access to computers, usually more than one, that we employ for both personal and professional uses. The personal computer has empowered people in ways unimaginable only a few years ago—to do good, and to do bad.

And somewhere along the line, God said, let there be an

Internet. Actually, it was the Defense Advanced Research Projects Agency (DARPA) that developed the Internet in 1974, at first as a secretive means for scientists and researchers to share information. But it quickly went viral as it exploded across the globe.

"The telephone was a pervasive technology, but the Internet is the most pervasive thing we have ever dealt with," said my good friend and longtime colleague John Grimes, who served as Chief Information Officer under both President George Bush and Barack Obama. "I don't care if you are in WalMart or flying over the Pacific Ocean, your life is tethered."

Yes it is. The Internet brings people and organizations together all over the world instantaneously. It empowers people, organizations and nations, and it also poses real threats to people, organizations and nations"

By 1991, the Internet had morphed into the Worldwide Web. The web as it exists today is a veritable "wild west" of information technology run amok. Most of us use it for sensible, legal purposes, but its potential for misuse and abuse is virtually unlimited. Probably 90 percent of information traffic on the Internet today is bogus in one form or another—from spam to identity theft to viruses to actual cyber attacks—designed to disrupt national economies, shut down electricity grids, or pillage financial institutions. Every government and every international company or organization must spend huge sums to defend its communications networks. There are many bad actors out there who are constantly seeking ways to take advantage of the new technologies to our detriment. Our government is being challenged as never before to protect our interests from invisible but potent threats in cyberspace. And of course, a major part of that focus is on the military which must protect us from foreign attacks.

Threat or no threat, the pell-mell race to communications

chaos is on. There are more cell phones in the U.S. today than there are people. I have not figured out why that is except to observe that we are embarked upon a global riot of communications technology that is both straining our ability to decipher the tide of information and threatening to overwhelm out ability to deal with it.

There is theoretically no limit to how much communication cable we can lay under the sea, or from town to town, but up above we are running out of room for satellites. Already, the space station has been rerouted a few times to avoid collision with errant satellites. We are also seeing the limits of bandwidth to support all of this chatter. The government needs a major portion of that bandwidth to support military, national security and civilian emergency needs. Educational institutions need more and more of it for online learning programs. The private sector needs more of it for more cable TV service, more cell phones, more everything. These competing interests are being fought out in Congress during increasingly acrimonious hearings and debates.

Perhaps one of the most interesting aspects of the new digital communications age is the spectacle of China's government trying to regulate the flow of information among its 1.3 billion people. I fully understand Beijing's desperation. It has scant legitimacy and its increasingly educated population will not indefinitely tolerate unresponsive government. But I do not believe the Chinese government can control this technology indefinitely. It has a power of its own and is moving ahead heedless of any government's concerns. What I know of history suggests big changes are coming to China in the not too distant future.[3]

My more immediate concern is the changes that are coming

---

[3] China is also engaged in wholesale industrial espionage to steal our intellectual property, a recurring bone of contention between our governments.

to my country—in terms of national security, economic development and cultural evolution. I am particularly interested in the potential of using advanced, interactive digital technology to improve our education training for both military and civilian applications. I helped set up a system to provide hands-on training to National Guardsmen and Reservists in their home communities, reducing travel costs and making more advanced training available to more people. I see a tremendous potential for this system, or one like it, to help improve public schools. But we have not begun to realize the full potential of that technology, and our children are suffering for it. If we don't get ahead of it, our nation's future will be imperiled.

The communications revolution offers great potential to improve humanity, but also power to do great harm. It is imperative that we recognize these challenges and act responsibly to meet them. To do that, we must first gain understanding of the dynamics of the revolution now underway—where we were, where we are now and where we are going. For me it has been an exciting lifelong journey, but I have yet a few miles to go before I sleep.

CHAPTER 3

Off To War In Korea

Nothing in life is so exhilarating as to be shot at
without result.
—Winston Churchill

WHEN I WAS GRADUATED FROM WEST POINT IN 1952, THE
Korean War was raging and there was no question I would end up
in combat. But first things first. I had met my wife to be, Barbara
Jamison, the year before. We were married upon my graduation
in June at her family's home in Jeannette, Pennsylvania. We had a
brief honeymoon at a lodge in West Virginia, after which I reported for a short basic Signal Corps course at Fort Monmouth, New
Jersey, from July through September.

Immediately after that I was sent for further training at
Camp San Luis Obispo in California and that in itself was something of an adventure. You did not whiz back and forth from
coast to coast on jetliners back in those days. Barbara and I drove
across the country in my 1946 Packard. It did not offer much in
the way of comfort or amenities, but that engine—the same as
was used in LST landing craft in World War II—would outrun
anything on the road, except possibly a gas station. We covered
600 hundred miles a day.

I should interject here that in those days there was a rule that
graduates of West Point should have at least six months in-country before they were shipped out to a war zone. The graduates

of previous classes sent directly into battle had been pretty badly chewed up. So I did not go directly to war.

We rented a little place overlooking the Pacific Ocean at Shell Beach, leaving me a 20 mile ride to the base. We had no money but there were many wonderful places to see, and we spent many hours walking along the beach watching the western sun settle beneath the waves. I don't believe we could have had a more joyful honeymoon anywhere else. But we were there only a few months. By March 1953, Barbara was pregnant and I had my orders for Korea where the war was still raging amid rumors of a possible truce. She went home to her family in Jeannette and I took my place in a long line of second lieutenants headed for the war zone.

We spent 17 days on a troop ship—one of the old Liberty ships left over from World War II. The creature comforts were few, but we had mostly good weather which was the main thing. A churning sea can cause extreme discomfort for a troop ship where several hundred men are crammed into tight places. But we had fair sailing and they allowed us ample time on deck to get some sun and fresh air. That old tug had a couple of guns on the forward deck, but that was mostly for show. The North Koreans had no submarines. There was no war on the Pacific during the Korean conflict.

We first touched land in Japan at Yokohama, southeast of Tokyo, which was a major staging area for the Korean War. At that time, Japan was still devastated by the bombings of World War II, and most of us military personnel were still steeped in anti-Japanese sentiment. In any event, I was not there long and did not get to see much of the country or interact with the people. They quickly moved us west to the port of Sasebo where we embarked on a smaller vessel for a short sail to Pusan, South Korea. A few hours later we marched down the gangplank without fanfare into a war zone that was still raging hot. The major dramas of that conflict that we now read about in history books—the heroic Marine retreat from the Chosin Reservoir, MacArthur's brilliant amphibious landing at Inchon—were over. The war had evolved into a stalemate of opposing lines rather like the trenches of World War I. What remained were continual mortar attacks by both sides, raids under cover of darkness, sporadic exchanges of artillery and machine fire and an occasional all-out battle over some now-forgotten hill.

I was assigned to the 45th Division, which was the Oklahoma National Guard. On our left was the 40th Division, the California National Guard. We were fighting on the east central front where some of the most intense combat took place. I had been assigned to the Signal Corps, which was where I would spend my military career, but as a West Point graduate I was also qualified in infantry. I was on occasion sent out leading patrols into hot zones, but was not qualified to wear the infantryman's badge. I packed grenades, the customary .45 caliber standard issue sidearm and also an M-2 carbine with a bayonet. I was also qualified to use a Thompson machine gun with a drum ammunition feed like you see in those gangster films of the 1930s. It was a good weapon that saw a lot of use in WWII and Korea. We used it for protection of crypto vans that would have been extremely valuable to the enemy had they been captured. I learned to shoot it, but I never had occasion to actually use it in combat. We also had a "grease" gun available when we were on crypto van duty, and I learned to shoot it too, but I frankly found that thing difficult to handle. It would kick right out of your hands when you fired it. I figured if I got in a fight with that thing I would just throw it at the enemy. Fortunately it did not come to that.

Which is not to suggest I was not in the thick of things and that I and my comrades were not in harm's way. In fact, one of my former West Point roommates, Dick Shea, who arrived in

Korea about the same time I did, lost his life in hand-to-hand combat with the enemy in a well-publicized fight at Pork Chop Hill. Dick was a man of solid values and strong religious conviction. We shared a double bunk, with him on top. I did not need an alarm clock because every morning at 5:30 he was up and about, getting dressed on his way to Mass. He was a superior athlete, a track star at West Point, and could have competed in the 1952 Olympics, but he chose instead to serve his country. I recall, when we were cadets, I would come back to our room and find him doing handstands on the arm of a chair. He had natural athletic ability, a pleasant personality and absolute integrity—a fine man all around. His death was keenly felt by all of us who knew him. His bravery in his last fight was conspicuous. He was later awarded the Congressional Medal of Honor.

Most of my work in Korea, befitting a Signal Corps officer, was spent running communication wires between the front lines and command posts in the rear. We had walkie talkies, but they were FM radios that really depended on line of sight to work properly. They will not carry signals over a mountain, and Korea is just one mountain after another. Generally speaking, if you don't have line of sight with the other party, your walkie talkie will not work very well.

Good communications of course are absolutely essential to effective coordination of military action on the battlefield—calling in air strikes and artillery, moving support troops to where they are needed, calling for medical assistance and supplies, letting the commanders know what the real situation is. The enemy appreciates the vital function of communications and does what it can to disrupt it—including shoot at people like yours truly scurrying back and forth, repairing broken communication wires, keeping the phones working.

We started out with single strands of wire that quickly became bundled with many others until we had massive steel cables 6-8 inches thick. They were heavy and hard to manage. You could scarcely pick up a 10-foot section. We did not have time to bury them. We ran them along beside the road and through the trees. They looked like a bunch of spaghetti in the bushes, but they worked. Every time an enemy shell struck one, we had to splice it all back together in a hurry, sometimes under fire. That was when I really earned my pay.

When I wasn't running communication wires, I was leading patrols. The mosquitoes ate us alive and there was nothing to be done about it. Whether running wire or patrolling the perimeter, it was all uphill. Logic insists that some of it must have been downhill, but I only remember the uphill, always carrying heavy things, being tormented by mosquitoes and harassed by enemy fire. All day and all night you hear the whomp, whomp, whomp of artillery and mortar fire. We quickly learned to discern the sound of their artillery coming in from the sound of ours going out.

I led platoons repeatedly into an area we called "smoke valley" because we had to wait until we could lay down a smoke screen to conceal our movements, otherwise the enemy would walk mortar fire right on top of us. I was trying to do two jobs at once, protect my people and set up communications. Our purpose was to prevent infiltrators from sabotaging our communications equipment. A signal officer is constantly on the go trying to locate everyone, assure integrity of communication lines and keep the fighting men in touch with the command center in a chaotic environment. It was in some ways a harrowing experience, but I gained experience and knowledge that would sustain me over a lifetime in the military.

It was strictly tactical communications, telling headquarters what was going on and where to direct artillery fire. The theme was the same as in all wars, the basic timeless doctrine of putting steel on the enemy, killing as many of them as you can.

On the front lines, we had 240 mm cannon trained on the

North Korean/Chinese lines that were working night and day. A 240 mm cannon makes a lot of noise when it fires and even more when it hits. At night we had searchlights that would illuminate the Chinese and Korean trenches. The Chinese and Koreans would try to shoot out the lights as our artillery rained destruction on them. This was almost a nightly event, a regular Fourth of July fireworks display every time.

Another nightly event was a character we called "Bedcheck Charlie," a North Korean pilot in a little scout plane who came flying over almost every night. He did not drop much in the way of ordnance on us. I assume his purpose was mainly harassment, but those visits became something of a comic relief.

In a battlefield situation, you are always dirty, even if you are not actually locked into the line of fire in a trench or established combat position. It gets wearisome when you can't stand to be around yourself because you stink. But you might drive 10 miles down an old dirt road to get a shower, and by the time you got back you were as dirty as when you went. After a while, you more or less get used to it.

I slept on the ground sometimes, under a tent if one was available, in the open if not. It was usually wet and cold so we tried to find shelter to catch a little rest amid the drumbeat of artillery. I also served as liaison officer to a Greek regiment that was sleeping on the ground, so when I was with them at night-time, I slept on the ground with them.

The Philippine 14th Battalion Command Team was assigned to the 45th Division when I was with it, and along with them came a foreign West Point classmate of mine, Lopey Romado, with whom I had a close rapport. We conducted some serious commercial transactions with the Filipinos as we swapped them some plywood they needed to build shelter in return for some San Miguel beer which we needed to build character.

One thing you don't get from photos of battlefields is the

stink. Some action shots will capture the drama and films will give you some of the noise, but nothing conveys the smell. On a battlefield, you have men fighting each other to the death with guns and grenades and sometimes knives, wallowing in mud for days on end in an environment of sheer misery and horror. To me, the smell was the worst part of it. The pungent aroma of human excrement and rotting corpses would knock a buzzard off an outhouse.

Years later you remember the smell and the haunting specter of people at the very edge of human tolerance. The images you see are burned into your memory forever. I will never forget this one young soldier who had been on the line too long and had that vacant stare that soldiers acquire amid too much killing and dying. Someone had given him a tray of ice cream and it was just running off the plate as he stared vacantly off into space, in a trance.

A Signal Corps officer gets a lot of high level exposure very quickly, another interesting aspect of my career, and I have always had a way of assuming responsibilities beyond my rank. For example, the 45th Infantry received the Korean Presidential Citation, a medal we were entitled to wear. South Korean President Syngman Rhee made the presentation himself. Because I was managing the communications at the event, I ended up holding the microphone for President Rhee. There I was, a shavetail second lieutenant representing the United States at an event with a foreign head of state. As it happened, the message center was part of my platoon's responsibility. It was customary in the Signal Corps to run a second lieutenant through all the parts of a Signal Company—construction, radio, TTY (teletype) and photo, plus crypto, and I was no exception.

In a wartime environment, you quickly become very familiar with the media you have to work with. We had message center, teletype and wireless (which was radio teletype). We had air drop and delivery service in which light planes came in and either dropped a communications bag on the airstrip or flew between two lines with an extended hook that would snag the mail bag from the line. That worked fairly well except when there was wind and dust. In those days, we did not have copying machines. We had the old jelly roll (mimeograph) which was a messy way to reproduce things, but you make do with what you have.

And yes, we had carrier pigeons, but we used them only to send test messages. We had them in a cage at corps headquarters well to the rear. On at least one occasion, we drove them up near the front in Jeeps and put test messages in little capsules attached to them and set them free with instructions to fly back to headquarters. "Go that way," I said, pointing. Most of them made it, but we never actually had to use them to convey real time information. Pigeons were always the backup plan.

This was my first experience with pigeons and it was actually a little show we put on in the war zone to celebrate the anniversary of the Signal Corps. I recommended we get rid of them because they were expensive to feed and take care of and really served no purpose, but someone back in the states decided they were worth keeping and overruled me. (I was only a second lieutenant after all.) The pigeon program was finally disbanded in 1957.

Just a few months after I got to Korea, they signed the armistice on July 27, 1953. Any hopes I had of an early return home were dashed when the ruling came down that those of us in country only a little while, like me, would have to stay there longer. In fact, the armistice did not really signal the end of the fighting which continued sporadically for a long time. Korea was officially designated a combat zone up until 1954. And of course the infamous 38th parallel remains a dangerous area 60 years later, characterized by occasional encroachments and artillery attacks by the North Koreans. So we kept our heads down for a long time after July 27, armistice or no armistice.

Less than a month after the armistice, I got word that our daughter Barbara Lynn was born on August 22. I received the news with mixed joy and sadness—joy to learn that mother and daughter were doing fine, but sadness that I could not be there with them. Long separations are of course part and parcel of a military career, but the McKnights have managed to keep close to each other throughout most of my years in the Army—the exceptions being my stints in Korea, India and Vietnam.

I stayed with the 45th Division through December when it was rotated home, to be replaced by the 24th Division that had seen combat earlier and had been resting and refurbishing in Japan. I was assigned then to the 24th. It fell to me to turn over all the communications equipment of the 45th to the 24th, which proved to be an awesome undertaking. It must be remembered that the Army had arrived in Korea on short notice when the war broke out and had quickly pulled together equipment from a variety of sources. There were precious few technical manuals for the equipment we had. It worked because we had resourceful sergeants and warrant officers endowed with what we used to call Yankee ingenuity. When something did not work, they figured out how to make it work. They threw a lot of stuff together from whatever sources were available.

But I had to take inventory of everything we had, and that was one job that wore me out more than leading platoons under enemy fire. I was given two weeks to get as much of our communications wire as I could out of the Demilitarized Zone (DMZ). We were dealing with big bundles of steel wire that was highly coveted by the Koreans of both sides. They did not have much steel to work with in those days, and they could convert that wire into nails fairly easily.

On the day the armistice was signed, we were told to stop shooting at 2000 hours. We went into a shooting frenzy to unload a lot of extra ordnance right up to the bewitching hour. Then suddenly the landscape became deathly quiet. The war was over, or at least the shooting had stopped. We lost about 33,000 Americans killed in that "police action," and I have no idea how many Chinese and Koreans died. Many more wounded, of course. Certainly, nothing much changed. The border between North and South Korea remained about where it had been before the hostilities started, and North Korea remains an impoverished dictatorship to this day.

I should say that the only Koreans I personally got to know while I was there (I was not on first name terms with Syngman Rhee), were the kids and mamasans who followed us around doing our laundry and providing some native foods to spice up the standard infantrymen's diet. Most of these people saw us (I presume) as their meal tickets and were very loyal to us. But I spoke little Korean and have no idea what they thought of the political situation. As for the capital city of Seoul, it was a big rock pile. No one looking at that wasteland then could imagine it would become the modern, bustling city of today.

After signing over all of our communications equipment and infrastructure material to the 24th Division, I was shifted to the 3rd Division, a regular Army division, which was then posted in the Chorwon Valley on the eastern front, which had been a major thoroughfare throughout the war for communists coming south and United Nations forces moving north. By the time I got there, the armistice was taking hold and there was little shooting.

In those days, we had regiments, not brigades. The 3rd Division had three regiments and each regiment had four or five battalions, each of which might be composed of a cavalry squadron, a separate reconnaissance squadron and maybe with some extra artillery attached. We always had loads of artillery on hand, but as I say, by the time I got to the 3rd, most of the fighting was over.

I left Korea with the vivid impression we are living in a wired world because everything had to be wired together for the communications to work. The radios provided great service in some situations, but they were sporadic. After months of running around the hills of Korea, I figured if I was to ever be Chief Signal Officer (an office that existed at that time), I needed to get to graduate school and learn more about my chosen field.

I spent 14 months in the Korean theater itself, and three more in transit, bounding around here and there. I had been hoping to be reunited with Barbara and meet Lynn but no such luck. They sent me to the 3rd Division. But I had another option. I could have opted for an inter-theater transfer to Japan, which you can do after you have spent a certain amount of time in a specific area of operations like the Korean War zone. But I had no desire to go to Japan, partly because the country had been laid waste, and also because I had an attitude toward the Japanese that was probably characteristic of most Americans at that time. We had been fed a steady barrage of propaganda about Japanese atrocities for years during WWII, most of which later proved to be real enough. I was especially appalled by the Japanese treatment of prisoners. Though I had experienced no direct injury from the Japanese, the prejudice was there inside me. I like to think I have lived long enough to rise above such feelings. In any event, I decided to complete my tour of duty in Korea and return to the states to be reunited with my growing family, and continue my campaign to get into graduate school.

In later years, I was often amused by the reaction of other senior officers to the television program M.A.S.H., based on a novel about a medical unit in the Korean War that had a successful run of 11 seasons on CBS. The TV program actually lasted much longer than the war, which was fine with me. I truly believe real wars should be as short as possible. But the theme of the program, which is still aired in reruns, is one of free spirited young people chafing at the restraints of a military regimen.

That tends to grate on the nerves of some senior officers who have built their careers on the military culture. But I have always harbored a not-so-secret respect for the resourceful noncoms that do their duty despite the restrictive environment they are obliged to function within, and who find ways to solve problems outside standard protocols. They are, and have always been, the true strength of the U.S. Army.

My experience in Korea helped me work through a lot of confusion in my personal life about what is important and what is not, and to treasure the things that matter. As a military officer, I developed an abiding faith in the noncommissioned officers of the military, the can-do guys who find a way to work around problems and who get things done despite confused leadership and contradictory orders. And as a Signal Corps officer, I came back with the vivid impression that I lived in a wired world. It did seem to me at that time, given the technology we had, that things had to be physically wired together to work reliably. We had radios that worked great in some circumstances, but they were sporadic and unreliable. I knew we were beyond the era of carrier pigeons-but not all that far beyond.

After eighteen months in the Army, as I was preparing to leave Korea, they made me a First Lieutenant, right on schedule.

CHAPTER 4

First European Tour

The French will only be united under the threat of danger. Nobody can simply bring together a country that has 265 kinds of cheese.
—Charles de Gaulle

AFTER 17 MONTHS IN THE KOREAN COMBAT ZONE, I FINALLY got my orders to come home in 1954. I spent 17 days on a liberty ship, but then I was able to fly to Pittsburgh, rather than spend days on a troop train with all the responsibilities and headaches that entailed. That was a relief. Every time the train stopped, personnel would get off and it was the officers' responsibility to make sure they got back on. Some would have too much to drink and get into fights. An officer on a troop train always had his hands full. It was like herding cats.

Back in those days, air travel was considered something of a luxury. I was flying short hops on prop planes but it was still a lot faster than a train. I was soon reunited with Barbara and met my daughter Barbara Lynn.[4] I immediately fell in love with that little girl, an affection which abides to the present day. I was posted to Fort Monmouth in New Jersey as company commander of a Signal Based Maintenance Company, and the three of us McKnights took up our first formal residence together there in a rented house in Long Branch, New Jersey.

---

[4] Who for reasons grown dim in memory has always been known as Lynn.

My consuming ambition in those days was to get to graduate school, which I saw as key to my professional development. A graduate degree would not only stand me in good stead in terms of career advancement, but also in terms of understanding the complexities of communications technology which even then was going into a period of rapid transition. But in the Army, while you can state your preferences, greater powers decide where you will go, what you will do and when you will do it. I put my name in the hat, but it was made clear to me that advanced education would have to wait a while.

At Fort Monmouth, I had about 300 people reporting to me in the signal company that previously had been based in Atlanta. In theory, this group was supposed to be able to fix any communications equipment in a combat theater if called upon to do so. According to the Army's plans, when sent into action it would be supplemented by up to 1200 people from the host country who were trained in electronics. That, of course, assumed the host country had 1200 people trained in electronics, which I would later learn is not necessarily the case. I also had a Women's Army Corps (WAC), a platoon of Military Police and other groups as part of what was a composite battalion commanded by a Lieutenant Colonel who was a WWII veteran.

I quickly got caught up in Fort Monmouth politics. I was supposed to be training my people to work with real world communications equipment, but we had no real world equipment to train with. I was required to submit regular progress reports to Fort Monroe, and in my first report I said I could not train the company personnel because we did not have the facilities and equipment we needed. The equipment was in fact at the base, but the civilian maintenance people who controlled it were using it for their own purposes and would not allow us to use it. The Signal Corps has always had a close working relationship with civilian communications firms, so this situation was not unusual, but it made it impossible for me to do my job.

It was a problem. You can't just let military personnel loll around all day. They are mostly young men and the devil finds work for idle hands. So I had them fixing wheel barrows and tricycles for base personnel. They should have been repairing signal equipment like radios and test meters. I told my superiors the Army should never have sent that command to Fort Monmouth. Well, of course young lieutenants who want to get ahead in the Army are not supposed to file reports like that. Before long, I was summoned to the Monmouth Inspector General (IG) who advised me, sure enough, that I should not be filing reports like that. I stood my ground, insisting we could not do what we were expected to do in that situation, and that I would continue to file those reports for as long as that situation persisted. He said, well okay, we understand each other, or words to that effect.

Not long after that, I was called before the IG again, this time to answer a complaint by an enlisted man who said I would not permit him to wear his wedding ring. Actually, I had told the fellow he could not wear his wedding ring in his ear while on duty. Ear rings are fairly common these days, but not in the U.S. Army, and certainly not in the Army in 1954. I told the soldier I did not care if he wore it in his nose while off duty, but while on duty, it could not be in his ear. That event was written up in the post newspaper, which may have been the first time I made the papers.

They eventually gave me some signal tracing equipment that enabled me to implement at least some training. Not long after I left Fort Monmouth, the Army deactivated that unit. I surmise they had kept it going in case the conflict in Korea erupted again, but eventually thought better of it. I suppose it was for the best. I did not see any point in paying people to be trained if there was no way to train them.

I should interject here that throughout my military career, I have made it a point to make as many friends up and down the line as possible. Of course, every ambitious young officer tries to ingratiate himself with superior officers, which I did, but I also made it a point to get to know people below me in the pecking order. Over a long career, I would learn that the Army really depends on its noncoms and warrant officers to get things done. These are the people who listen obediently to the wise instructions from Mount Olympus, and then turn around, scratch their chins, and find ways to apply them to the real world. The wise young officer who wants to succeed will pay attention to these people, get to know them, earn their trust and learn to depend on them.

One such fellow was a warrant officer who had served with me in Korea, and was now posted to Fort Monmouth as a personnel officer. He could see my career was drifting, and so he helped me shift over to the Publications Agency. Because I had acquired tactical experience in the war, they wanted me to help write a field manual on aerial delivery of photographic equipment and photos to tactical airstrips—something I had actually done in Korea where we would have aircraft fly low between two poles and pick up containers of photographs hanging on wires stretched between them. It sounds dangerous, and I suppose it was, but often there was no room for an airstrip. We did it any number of times without incident.

At the Publications Agency, they made me the adjutant, or the "bag man," to the director, Colonel Sydney O. Davis, who had been the Division Signal Officer for General Maxwell Taylor during the Battle of the Bulge in World War II. (Taylor would later serve as Chairman of the Joint Chiefs of Staff, and still later as Ambassador to Vietnam.) Davis was a brilliant man with a mind like a steel trap. He taught ROTC at Northeastern University—which over the years has provided the Signal Corps with many of its finest officers. Colonel Davis had me write up certain points he would make when reporting to Washington, whether to superior officers at the Pentagon or to members of

Congress. We did not have Power Point in those days, but I worked up talking points and charts for him to use.

Davis's deputy Colonel Bill Frame was another savvy colonel who earned his spurs in WWII, and knew his way around. Frame was a reservist with a construction background, and was responsible for heavy construction at Fort Monmouth. Together, Davis and Frame imparted much of their experience to me. I learned a lot from them including how to navigate the labyrinth of senior Army brass, a lesson that would stand me in good stead over the years. They taught me a lot also about the politics of the Signal Corps and would spend hours making sure I knew who was on the rise and who was not. Davis and Frame were probably too old to make general, but they were highly competent and well respected officers. They advised me that the people in research & development were all bridge players. If I didn't play bridge, I would never make it with them. They warned me the people in procurement were sly and crafty, not to be trusted very far. And they told me it was the officers in the field, managing communications for Army units in action, who were the George Pattons of the Signal Corps, and who had the best chance of becoming generals. I took note of that.

I served those colonels in a variety of roles, including speech-writer and major domo for the Publications Agency which included many writers, cartoonists, and graphics experts. I not surprisingly learned a lot about publications when I was there. We had a big printing plant churning out tactical manuals that instructed enlisted personnel how to use our increasingly sophisticated communications equipment. The manufacturers supplied training manuals, but they needed people with actual combat experience, like yours truly, to translate those complicated documents into usable formats for real world application. We also handled photography and the infamous carrier pigeon program, which as I said was finally phased out in 1957.

Perhaps the most significant, or at least most memorable, event for me, during our time at Fort Monmouth, was the birth of our second daughter Marsha on May 28, 1955, which happened about the time I transferred to the Publications Agency. That was a wonderful time in my personal life. I was with my entire family for the first time, watching the little darlings learn to walk and talk. It was a rather unusual time in my career when I was able to live something close to a normal life, working during the day and coming home most evenings at dinner time.

There was a lot going on around us in those years. President Eisenhower was providing impetus for the Interstate Highway System, an idea which had been perking around for years but finally got Congressional backing. Eisenhower had been tasked to move a military unit across country during World War I. He had developed a belief that our patchwork of highways and byways were inadequate for a modern country—and he was right. The Interstate would dramatically remake the face of our nation, providing tremendous advances in economic growth and cultural mobility.

And then there was that box in the living room, one of the first generation of televisions that brought live entertainment into the homes of ordinary people like us for the first time. I remember sitting there on Saturday nights watching "Gunsmoke" and "Your Hit Parade," marveling at the transmission of sound pictures, and speculating what that advance in telecommunications might mean to the evolution of military communications. I had visions of providing commanders, not only with verbal reports of battlefield conditions, but actual real time pictures. I would live to see that vision fulfilled, but it would take a while.

There was a lot of mindless tripe on the TV screen in the early years of the industry, but also many excellent dramas and sophisticated comedies. I could not begin to guess where it would lead, but I could see the times were changing and it would have profound impact on the career I had chosen. Interestingly, the Chairman of the Federal Communications Commission under President Kennedy, Newton Minnow, would famously describe the fare offered on public TV in those days as "a vast wasteland." Today we refer to that period as the "Golden Age of Television."

This was the era of the great red scare when Senator Joe McCarthy (R-WIS) was leading a campaign to root out alleged communist sympathizers from all levels of government, including the military. For some reason, McCarthy had it in for the Signal Corps, and our senior officers were required to spend a lot of time defending themselves from spurious allegations of treasonous intent. I do not believe there was ever anyone in the Signal Corps who warranted such treatment, or indeed anyone in the U.S. Army who did, but that was something that had to run its course. McCarthy, of course, was eventually disgraced and his witch hunts finally came to an end, though people to this day still argue about whether it served a valid purpose.

Off to Europe

It was about this time that I got it into my head that I should leave the military and strike out on my own. I knew the telecommunications field was moving into a period of rapid change and that officers with my experience could expect to find lucrative opportunities in the private sector. Also, I was chafing at the bit to get into graduate school. Of course I would have had trouble making that happen on my own with a wife and two small children to support. I discussed this idea with Colonel Frame, who aggressively dissuaded me, insisting I had a great future in the Signal Corps. Within two weeks, I had orders to go to Europe. That got my attention; I had never been to Europe.

My first post was in France where I was assigned to the Supreme Headquarters Allied Powers Europe (SHAPE). Barbara and the girls came with me. We leased a beautiful house in Leroy in the suburbs of Paris and settled in for what I assumed would be an exciting and enlightening adventure. But it was cold in Paris, in more ways than one. The house had a marginal heating system, and the French people—at least the people in Paris—exhibited a conspicuous contempt for Americans. Also, the French drivers drove me to distraction. One day driving a car in Paris I stopped for some pedestrians who were jaywalking and got rammed by a city bus. The driver got out, looked at the car, looked at me, shrugged his shoulders and drove off. Every car in the SHAPE parking lot had dents. There was no way to avoid them, and no way to make errant drivers pay for the damage they did. The French were some of the craziest drivers I ever saw.

I had a smattering of French because my mother knew a few French phrases and had imparted them to me and my sister. So I could order croissants in a restaurant. We saw the Eiffel Tower, Notre Dame and other key Parisian sights, but never really got to know the city. I simply could not bridge the culture gap in Paris. The Cold War was heating up and there was a huge communist element in the French capital with strong anti-American sentiment. French President de Gaulle was doing all he could to keep France free of the Soviet orbit, but in deference to the anti-western mood in his country, he would eventually order SHAPE to get out. After that, as my friend General Colin Powell has said, the only Americans left were the caretakers of U.S. military cemeteries.

By the time that happened, we were already gone. Not long after we got to France, we discovered that Marsha had a malformed hip, with no head of one of her femurs. She simply could not walk. We took her to a medical facility in Orleans, outside of

Paris, and that trip was a revelation. Barbara and I got the distinct impression that people outside Paris in the countryside were very pro-American. They treated us exceedingly well, but they did not have the capability there to deal with Marsha's problem. We needed to take her to Germany where more advanced medical treatment was available.

I located a good hospital in Germany and applied for a transfer. But we had only been in France four months and my hardship request was frowned upon. I was reliably told by upper Signal Corps people in Washington that this decision would hinder my career, and that they could not give me a good job near the hospital that could take care of Marsha. I found that exceedingly discouraging, but told them my family came first—now and always. I would offer that advice to all young officers—or young people in any field for that matter—keep a balance in your life. Your career is important; your family is more important.

As it happened my transfer to Germany worked out well, and it obviously did not derail my career ambitions. We moved into a U.S. military housing area near Kaiserslautern west of the Rhine, the largest U.S. Army housing unit outside the U.S. We had two bedrooms on a second floor that was toasty warm in the bitter cold German winter. Marsha got the therapy she needed and was soon hobbling along with casts and braces. She had to deal with that for more than a year, as I recall, but she recovered completely and is today living a rich, full life. I like to say she got up one day and never sat down again.

We found Germany to our liking, and why not? A German beer cost about 7 cents a bottle back then, and it was great beer. I worked decent hours and got to spend many wonderful hours with my family. I had important work to do and the German people were as hospitable as the people of Paris were inhospitable.

I was assigned to Western Signal Command as an Area

Signal Officer where I reported to Colonel Dick Stillwell, who eventually became a four star general, and who would later serve as Assistant Secretary of Defense. They put me in charge of the telephone system for Western Germany that had originally been built by Hitler's government. I oversaw about 30 telephone exchanges which was a considerable responsibility. It was a dual use system for both civilians and the military. It was basic technology, but reliable. It was something we could build on and I would use it to great effect during future tours of duty in Germany.

One of the original mandates under the Marshall Plan was to stimulate older industries and get them going again, including their cable and switch companies. The Cold War was on in earnest, as evident in the anti-western mood in France, and we saw West Germany as a bulwark against Soviet expansionism. From the ashes rose Krupp, TBK, many industrial giants. One of the big German companies we worked with was Siemens, which is today one of the largest communications conglomerates in the world. I found myself going back and forth to Heidelberg frequently in my work to rebuild and upgrade the German communications system. I learned a lot about telephone technology during this time, knowledge that helped broaden my grasp of the overall telecommunications world.

Not long after we transferred to Germany, the entire SHAPE headquarters moved to Brussels, Belgium, when they were ordered out of France. (That may be one reason my transfer did not hamper my career aspirations.) After that, the Signal Corps had to come up with creative ways to bypass France with our communications back to the U.S. We were able to solve that problem. The U.S. commander of the Strategic Air Command for Europe (SACEUR), usually a four star Air Force general, was based in Stuttgart, Germany.

In 1957, the Soviets launched the first satellite to spin

around the globe—Sputnik—that threw our country into a tizzy. We had just been emerging from the "red scare" of the mid-50s, and the challenge of Sputnik brought it all back overnight. Only this time the concern was not communist sympathizers in high places, but rather a communist system that seemed to be passing us by in technology. Almost overnight, public schools and universities in the U.S. were putting great stress on science and technology studies. Not surprisingly, the Signal Corps, which had always been focused on developing advanced technologies, was getting a broader mandate and more resources.

Finally, in 1959 I got my orders to return to the U.S. to go to the University of Michigan for the graduate studies I had been lobbying for. I do not know if this had anything to do with the new emphasis generated by Sputnik. I do know some of the credit goes to a ringing endorsement from Brigadier General Kenneth Zitzman, who would later become head of personnel for the Signal Corps. I owe General Zitzman a debt of gratitude. I brought my wife and girls along with me. Daddy was off to college again.

CHAPTER 5

The Rockets' Red Glare

Once the rockets are up
who knows where they come down?
That's not my department,
says Werner von Braun.
                    —*Tom Lehrer*

I WAS INTENT ON FURTHERING MY EDUCATION IN PART TO advance my career in the Army, but also because I was cognizant that I was on the leading edge of a sea change in technology and needed more education to understand what was going on all around me. I had received an excellent education at West Point, but I sensed that too much of it was backward looking to the experiences of World War II, where many of our instructors had served with distinction. I cannot claim at that time that I foresaw the looming revolution in digital communications, but I knew whatever was coming would be based on electricity. Ergo, I sought to acquire an advanced degree in electrical engineering.

Most people tend to think of water and electricity as basic components of our residences and workplaces. If you have a problem with the water, you call a plumber. If you have a problem with the electricity, you call an electrician. But the reality is that water and electricity are totally different animals. I would liken water to a trusty dog that is totally predictable. All you need to really know about plumbing is that water runs downhill. You can send it through a conduit five feet or five miles long, and if it's downhill and unclogged, the water will go its merry way. Electricity is more like a cat—you just never know what it's going to do. You can't just send it in a straight line for any distance because of something called flux that will block transmission. It is a natural phenomenon. Telephone poles have multiple cross arms with little glass insulators mixing the lines so they cross at different angles, up and down. That convoluted system bends the path of the electricity and cancels the flux out—if you do it right.

That's the thing about electricity—you better do it right the first time. You can get the water lines wrong and end up getting wet. If you get the electricity lines wrong, you can end up getting fried. We lose a lot more people to electricity than we do to water lines. And when you are relying on electricity for communications, you have to understand the science of the beast and know how to manage it—especially when you are bouncing signals off the moon or following the trajectory of intercontinental ballistic missiles.

So I brought my young family with me to the University of Michigan. Actually, we could not afford to live in Ann Arbor where the university is because the rents were so high. Rather, we found a place in Ypsilanti, Michigan, a relatively low-rent community about six miles east of the school. I do not mean this to sound like a complaint. In fact, I was to spend about 18 months at the University earning my degree while drawing my captain's salary which, although modest, was sufficient for the four of us. We had food to eat, a roof over our heads and medical care, courtesy of Uncle Sam. At West Point and Michigan I got my compensation a nickel at a time. You can do alright in the military if you have patience.

I can say in candor that I did not waste Uncle Sam's money during that sojourn in Michigan. I cracked the books and I worked as hard as I have ever worked, often putting in 18-hour days. It was a rigorous curriculum that challenged my intellectual capacity to the fullest because I did not have the background from West Point that I needed for much of the curriculum. I scarcely saw Barbara and the girls during that time. If I wasn't in class, I was in the library, or chasing down instructors with questions or discussing challenging matters with classmates. One of my classmates, an Air Force officer named Ed White, who would later be the first guy to walk in space, gave me a tutorial on which classes I should take, and warned me about which professors to avoid—because they had an anti-military bias. Then as now, there is a small but distinct anti-military tide in the rarified ranks of academia. Ed died in 1967 along with fellow astronauts Gus Grissom and Roger Chaffee in an accident at Cape Kennedy during a pre-launch test for the first manned Apollo mission. He was a great guy and a true American hero.

The University of Michigan was, and I assume still is, a rich intellectual environment. In those days, it was a major proving ground for astronauts, like Ed White, and was doing advanced work for the U.S. government through what was at the time called Project Michigan. (There are different programs using that title these days.) Based at Willow Run, an airport near Detroit, Project Michigan brought together a large military and academic group to do the heavy thinking about our part in the nuclear arms race, particularly with regard to command and control of missile sites. We were at the time engaged in an arms race often referred to as MAD (mutually assured destruction) with the Soviet Union. The basic idea, and one simple enough for everyone to grasp, was that if you destroy us, we will destroy you too, even as our civilization goes up in mushroom clouds. We had basically three launch platforms for nuclear warheads just in case the Soviets were to launch a preemptive strike against us: nuclear submarines, nuclear aircraft bombers (B52s) that were kept aloft continuously, and eventually land-based intercontinental ballistic missiles (ICBMs) in hardened silos virtually immune to attack. The Soviets, of course, had their own doomsday strategy in place to counter ours. Together, the Soviet Union and the United States were poised to launch enough destructive power to virtually wipe out humanity. There is still enough nuclear weaponry out there to accomplish that, but we don't think about it as much as we used to. We are more concerned about terrorism, but then if some terrorists get control of nuclear weapons...

To some extent, the knowledge I was acquiring, and the willingness of the Army to pay for it, was an outgrowth of the Cold War. But there was more to it than that. It had become a matter of national pride. In 1957, the Soviets had launched the first satellite into space, the Sputnik, that knocked our country on its collective ear. All of a sudden, it seemed like we were losing out in our competition with the Soviet Union. Overnight we had a national mandate at all levels to ratchet up our commitment to the hard sciences, make a fresh commitment to advanced technologies, and catch up with our Soviet rivals.

In April 1961, the Soviets scored another coup when they launched the first astronaut, actually a cosmonaut, named Yuri Gagarin, into space orbit. President Kennedy responded to that challenge the following month when he offered forth an ambitious plan, in an address to the Congress, to put a man safely on the moon by the end of the decade. All of a sudden the space race was on in earnest, culminating in the 1969 moon landing.

All of this was going on around me while I was hitting the books at Michigan. I was working so hard because I wanted to learn as much as I could. I stuck it out and got the master's degree in electrical engineering that enabled me to pull the curtain back and see the Wizard of Oz pulling the ropes. I can say at this late date that all of that hard work paid off. I took courses that put me in the vanguard of our nation's quest for the stars, and carried me right into the 21st century. I also developed an appetite for continuous learning that I retain until the present time. I never let a day go by without learning something, even if, as is often the case, it is something I really don't want to know.

White Sands

The moment I completed my studies and won my degree in 1961, the Army posted me to The Signal Missile Support Research and Development Agency at White Sands, New Mexico, just a few miles north as the crow flies from El Paso, Texas. Barbara and the girls came with me. Lynn was 8 and Marsha 6, so they were both in school by that time. There was a wonderful swimming pool there and they both took to the water like ducks, acquiring an affinity for aquatics that they never lost. It really was an ideal place to be after the graduate school grind I had been through and compared to the Michigan weather where it seems it is always raining or snowing.

Not for the first time, the Army put me in a position of responsibility above my rank. I was a captain serving in a lieutenant colonel's slot. Officially, I was a Department Chief over Electronics Research and Development. In fact, I was wearing two hats, one as director of the Automated Data Processing (ADP) department, and the other as security officer for the Electronic R&D Agency (ERDA). It was there that I first began to wrap my brain around the power of computers, and for the first time to grasp their implications for the future. I was under the command of an older infantry colonel, a holdover from WWII, who seemed baffled by the changing technology he was responsible for. He said to me, "Mac, get down there with those squirrels in the ADP department and figure it out. I can't understand what they are doing or why they are doing it."

What they were doing, I soon figured out, was charging headlong into a new world that would forever alter the way we live and work. Our primary mission at White Sands was to calculate the trajectories of missiles, and to compute the effect of weather on them. When you are firing missiles, it is important to know where—or approximately where—they will land. My master's degree in electrical engineering did not help me much in this, but I had taken some courses in computers, an emerging technology then in is formative stage, and so I was not intimidated when I was introduced to the Philco 2000.

That computer, an early prototype, filled an entire room with whirring tapes and blinking lights like something out of an early science fiction movie. It was mainly transistor based, though there may have been a few vacuum tubes here and there. Today, you could probably put all of that computing capability on your wrist, but at the time it was cutting edge. That computer was asynchronous, in that it was driven by functions and could perform several unrelated calculations at the same time. I was awed by the power of the thing and could imagine it being used in a variety of applications.

I was the Army contracting officer's representative for the Philco 2000, in which role I reported to both the Army and Philco. It was a new creature in the Army's arsenal. A good many older officers, like the colonel I reported to, did not understand computers and had no vision of what they would become. The Pentagon had allocated a lot of money for that thing and wanted to know if it was getting its money's worth. The Philco company representatives also were eager to learn how we were using it and whether we were satisfied with it. In that role, I was required to come to Washington, D.C., several times, which was for me an otherworldly experience. Up until that time, I had managed to avoid the beltway morass, and I would subsequently strive to avoid it in the future with some success until late in my career. When I was in Washington, the Philco people were constantly pressing me to join them out on the town for dinner, drinks and entertainment. I am sociable enough, but made it clear I could accept no gratuities—and I didn't. (The entertainment, by the way, was rather tame, at least by today's standards.)

The Army had a major installation in Huntsville, Alabama, where a team of scientists were developing the Redstone rockets that were laying the groundwork for intercontinental ballistic missiles then on the drawing board, and still later the rockets that would lift astronauts into outer space and on to the moon. The work we were doing factored into their calculations, and I was excited to be part of it.

One of the most famous rocketeers was Werner von Braun, the German scientist whom we had captured, along with several other scientists, in the waning days of WWII. Von Braun had earned more than a little notoriety by designing the V-2 "buzz bombs" that Adolph Hitler used to terrorize London during the war, and was reliably accused of using slave labor to help build them. But within the context of the Cold War, we needed his knowledge and expertise to counter that of the Soviets who had absconded with more than a few German scientists of their own. By most accounts, von Braun was a pivotal figure in the development of rocket technology for both Germany and the United States. I would have to say our decision to employ his talents was a wise one, despite his checkered past.

I found myself going back and forth to Alabama during my tenure at White Sands as our work progressed, talking to scientists about controlling missiles. I never actually met von Braun, I was a lowly captain after all, but I did see him a couple of times. He lived long enough to help us get to the moon. He died in 1977.

When I was in White Sands, there was a lot of missile testing going on all around me, and I was deeply involved in it.

Mostly they were prototypes of the ICBMs we were developing at the time to carry nuclear warheads deep into the Soviet Union if we needed to. Some of the missile development, as I said, was done in Huntsville. White Sands was strictly a test range. Today, there is a huge installation of the National Aeronautics and Space Administration (NASA) based there, and New Mexico State University is nearby. Then and now, there is a lot of brain-power amid those desert dunes.

We would fire missiles up 100,000 feet or more and track them, taking into account the winds aloft, and then explode metallic chaff that could be tracked with radar. (This data was collected at Fort Churchill in Canada.) We were capturing a lot of data on the speed and density of winds, and also the moisture content, to determine the trajectory of the missiles and the effect of weather conditions, particularly wind and moisture, on the transmission of electronic commands to the missiles. There was a group of scientists there representing all relevant fields, including mathematicians, who analyzed the data we provided.

We spent a lot of time analyzing the weather, which histori-cally had been one of the Signal Corps main functions. The impact of the weather, especially moisture, on electronic com-munications was always a major focus of our interest. We had a big pipe with a fan at one end into which we injected water, sim-ulating raindrops of different sizes, to see what the effect would be on electronic signals. You could see whether a radar beam would bend more or less depending on the size of the drops, and the different impact on different frequencies. I learned that if we could send a beam through the rain, it meant the signal was attenuating. You can penetrate mist or fog fairly easily, but rain is a bigger issue. I also learned that in the final analysis, we sim-ply cannot predict the weather. Anyone who relies on the local forecast provided by local TV knows how unreliable that science is even today. Only God knows what the weather is going to do, and sometimes I doubt he can figure it out.

I soon began to realize how critical that fledgling computer was to the work we were doing. It could perform complicated calculations in seconds that would take humans weeks or months, and it did not make mistakes like humans do. Some of that technology was over my head, but I understood my job—to keep the money flowing from Washington. I narrowed it down to three projects where it was clear to me we were accomplishing important work: analyzing weather patterns, tracking the missiles and assessing their impact with acoustical sound-all of it backed up by computer analysis.

Using our photo lab, I made up some impressive multi-colored charts, which was more of a challenge in those pre-Power Point days than it is today. This was an educational experience for me learning how to direct the research and development process in a positive way, using what were essentially "Dick and Jane" visual representations. Young leaders on the rise take note—this is especially important when you are trying to explain complicated information to generalists who do not fully grasp what you are talking about. If the generalists are senior Army officers, the problem is even more complicated. You cannot confront such people with their ignorance. But well thought out, carefully prepared charts can convey concepts more readily than mere words. This education would stand me in good stead many years later when, as a three star Lieutenant General, I was called upon to explain complex communications issues to senior government officials, including cabinet officers, who often had no idea what I was talking about.

A sideline of my time at White Sands—and a theme that would repeat itself in my career over and over in the years to come—was my contemptuous treatment of secret records. Then as now, the Army routinely classified just about anything as secret. I eliminated huge amounts of allegedly secret records at

White Sands because they were worthless and it cost too much money to protect them.

White Sands gave me my first real world exposure to serious research & development, and imbued me for the first time with a sense that I would be able to use the knowledge I had acquired at the University of Michigan to support a successful career in the Army. In fact, I did so well with that Philco 2000 that senior personnel people in the Signal Corps chain of command wanted to shift me over to ADP (computers) permanently. I employed all of my wiles and contacts to avoid that fate. I knew it was an important field, but I also knew that the people who went there became known as "geeks" and few ever escaped. Certainly, none that I knew of became general officers. I wanted a bigger career than that, and did not wish to be pigeonholed as a computer geek.

Others at Signal Corps high command wanted to post me to West Point to teach, whether electrical engineering or computer technology. They had paid for my graduate degree and expected me to share my knowledge with cadets. That assignment I resisted even more assiduously. Teaching at West Point is important, and if you enjoy teaching it can make for a satisfying and rewarding career. But if you aspire to become a general officer, and I did, teaching at West Point is a dead end. I know of few who have taken that assignment and ended up wearing stars. Most of my social friends in the military have always been in the infantry or artillery, not the Signal Corps, and certainly not in ADP. Had I gone into ADP, I would have been closeted.

I was supposed to be at White Sands for three years, but was there less than two. The Army had other plans for me. For reasons I never quite understood, they wanted me to go to India. The Chinese had launched an attack on India, and we were sending a joint military-diplomatic mission to show moral support for India without getting involved in the shooting. Barbara and I had a brief panic when we thought I was going to have to leave immediately, but the usual Army paperwork got bogged down long enough for us to get her and the girls off to a civilian housing unit, Cielo Vista Apartments, near Ft. Bliss and the El Paso airport, where I knew they would be welcomed by other military families. I went on to India alone.

CHAPTER 6

Off To India

*India is a geographical term. It is no more a united
nation than the equator.*
—Winston Churchill

IN JANUARY 1963, I WAS SENT ON A MISSION THAT I WOULD
describe as both military and political—to India which had been
defending itself against an invasion by China that began in late
1962. I cannot explain why I was chosen for this assignment,
because no one ever explained it to me. I can only surmise that
I had impressed some of the higher ups as a junior officer with
sound judgment. I was only a captain at the time, but even then
I was routinely being posted to jobs that were normally assigned
to people two or three ranks above me, and I never complained
about it. I suppose that commended me also. As I would learn
for myself eventually, senior officers appreciate junior officers
who accept their assignments without complaint.

Still, I found it interesting to be assigned to what was both a
military and diplomatic mission. Many young officers are exu-
berant and ambitious, as I was, and more than a little aggressive.
But while you expect aggressiveness in military leaders of whatever rank, some assignments demand a more balanced tone and
sense of decorum. I can be as tough as anyone when the circumstances call for it. For example, when I was based in Germany in
the post-Vietnam period, and drug abuse was rampant among

military personnel, I put down the hammer hard, ending more than a few careers. But normally I am civil and inclined to get along with people from other walks of life—be they part of the cultural mix that characterizes the U.S. military or people from other countries and backgrounds.

The people I was to meet in India were definitely from other walks of life. Then and now, India is a fascinating country of astounding contrasts—great wealth and beauty amid some of the most heartbreaking poverty I have ever seen; extraordinary culture built upon millennia of intellectual advances adrift in a sea of illiteracy and appalling ignorance; and a challenging diversity of climate ranging from arid deserts to dense jungles to vast wetlands to frozen peaks at the roof of the world—the Himalayas. It's all there. Anything you might care to say about India is probably true.

As fate would have it, my work in India was mostly in the Himalayas where the Chinese and Indians had been fighting. It was not clear then, and is not much clearer today, what that conflict was all about. At issue was a muddled border dispute regarding where the boundary between China and India actually was. The question had never been resolved mainly because there was little reason to. It was forbidding terrain about 16,000 feet above sea level where the air is thin and few people live year round. There is no commerce, agriculture or mining of consequence. I can tell you based on personal experience that the first human reaction to that environment is to want to go somewhere else as quickly as possible. It is bitter cold the year round and merely breathing up there is a major challenge.

The Chinese believed, and not without reason, that the Indians were encroaching on their territory. The Indian government of Prime Minister Jawaharlal Nehru had been pursuing what it called a "Forward Policy" on a number of fronts, asserting Indian sovereignty over disputed lands, especially in the former Portuguese colony of Goa on the southwest coast of India. A number of Indian leaders asserted that if China did not abandon disputed lands on their common border, India would act against China as it did with Portugal over Goa.

The Chinese took note of that threat. "Nehru's forward policy is a knife," said Chinese Foreign Minister Chen Yi. "He wants to put it in our heart. We cannot close our eyes and await death."

Of course, India never posed a serious security threat to China and the border land in the Himalayas dispute was of no practical use to anyone. On a more fundamental level, some analysts believe the Chinese probably viewed India's alleged incursions as part of a Soviet-U.S.- Indian effort to encircle and isolate their country. Actually, though India was close to both the Soviet Union and the U.S. at that time, the U.S. and the Soviet Union were embroiled in the Cuban Missile Crisis, probably as close to open warfare that we ever were. That the Soviets, the U.S. and India would be in cahoots against China over some God-forsaken frozen wastelands in the Himalayas may strike us as a bizarre notion, but paranoia runs deep and the Chinese have always had their own way of looking at things.

In any event, there were several outbreaks of fighting between Chinese and Indian border troops in the summer of 1962, and in October the Chinese launched two attacks about a thousand miles apart, one in Ladakh, India's arctic-like district in Kashmir, and the other in the North East Frontier Agency, at the far end of India's 1,500 mile barrier with Tibet. I was to spend some time in Ladakh which is one of the world's highest inhabited lands. It does not dip below 6,000 feet altitude even in its lowest valleys. Goatherds living at 18,000 feet suffer discomfort when they descend to Leh, the capital city, which is only 11,500 feet above sea level. It is really like going to another planet in more ways than one.

It is terrible country to wage war in—which is not to suggest that any country is good for waging war. The Indian army was at a disadvantage using outdated weapons from World War II and endowed with virtually non-existent communications. By the time the Indian military leaders found out what was happening on the frontier, it was over and the damage was done. It was yet another stark reminder to me of how vitally important communications are to any military operation, and how incredibly difficult the most minimal communications can be in a hostile environment like the Himalayas. Overall, the Indians got the worst of it and I believe most of the disputed territory ended up in Chinese hands.

But it took a while for all of that to play out and the U.S. could not just sit back and allow China to invade our ally India without doing something. President John F. Kennedy was adamant that we should make a measured response-enough to remind the Chinese that we supported India without provoking a military confrontation that would require a major U.S. military commitment.

Kennedy had a lot on his mind in those days. There was great debate whether he was a hawk or a dove, terms that routinely flew around back during the Cold War. Kennedy's main adversary, Nikita Khrushchev, had taken measure of our young President and decided he was a pushover. The next thing you know the Soviets were setting up nuclear missile launch pads in Cuba. After some very scary brinksmanship, Kennedy cut a deal with the Soviets, agreeing to remove our missiles from Turkey in exchange for the Soviets removing theirs from Cuba. But it was a tense time that left many people shaken. So when the Chinese invaded India, Kennedy was dealing with the aftermath of the Cuban Missile Crisis and was even then being sucked into the Vietnam quagmire. The last thing he wanted at that juncture was to be dragged into yet another open-ended commitment in India.

So I was part of a military-diplomatic team sent to India to provide the Indians with some military support without overdoing it, enough to help a little and let the Chinese know there was a commitment there of some kind. This is what some would call "soft power." I did not know how long I would be there, but figured it would be a while. After about six months in India, the situation appeared stable enough for some of us to bring our families over to New Delhi. I could have brought Barbara and the girls to stay with me, but I thought better of it. I had never been to India, but I had heard a lot about it and was reluctant to plunk my young family down in such a strange and unfamiliar environment. So I left them in El Paso, Texas, where I assumed they would all do well. Many Army officers off on tours to Vietnam or other hot spots would leave their families in El Paso. Barbara had a car, there was an Army post there with a commissary, and many of the school kids were military brats like Lynn and Marsha. They enjoyed this sojourn in El Paso.

My family would be with me on the great majority of my assignments around the world in years to come, but not that one. Looking back, I think that was one of my more judicious decisions. There are many new and unfamiliar ways to get hurt in India—tigers, elephants, fetid water, crazy drivers, wild-eyed gurus, leprosy and some of the world's deadliest snakes - to name a few. I needed to have my wits about me on that trip, and did not want to be worrying all day about my family.

This is not meant in jest. I can recall more than one incident when I was traveling with colleagues in the Indian military that the driver would suddenly swerve off the road into a culvert or some other protected area to avoid a group of elephants that had suddenly appeared out of nowhere. They try to keep the elephants on wildlife preserves, but elephants pretty much go when and where they please. On one occasion, I was advised we were avoiding a "rogue" elephant, which can be especially unpredictable, but I have made it a lifetime habit to stay out of the way of elephants of whatever disposition.

We had drivers to take us where we wanted to go, but for no particular reason I insisted on getting my own Indian driver's license. That was an experience I should not like to repeat in this lifetime. We have bureaucracy here—and the Department of Motor Vehicles is generally ranked among the worst—but the Indian bureaucracy is in a league by itself. It took me many long days of waiting in lines and arguing about trifles, but I finally got my license. It was about two feet wide and three feet long, covered with stamps and signatures.

An Indian driver's license is not something you tuck away into your wallet. But it did leave me with one lesson—regardless of what country you are in, the Department of Motor Vehicles is always the same.

Because we were supposed to play down our military connections, I was instructed to take a good supply of civilian clothes along. That was a bit of a problem. Almost all of my clothes were military uniforms, and as a lowly captain, my salary did not provide for things like civilian clothes that I had little occasion to wear in the U.S. I knew I needed lightweight clothing because the climate in New Delhi is very hot and humid. On the other hand, it was like Antarctica up in the Himalayas where the action was. Barbara bought me a couple of seersucker suits, which was a fine idea, but did not really meet the challenge of India. I mean it gets seriously hot in some parts of that country. When seersucker material gets too hot, it just melts like plastic.

It does get hot over there—really hot—like about 110 degrees on a regular basis, and humid too which makes the world seem like an oven. I would get up at 4 a.m. to go running when I was in New Delhi, but it was still over 100 degrees. I could not run very far in that heat, but I do remember admiring the multicolored peacocks I passed along the way. Wherever you are in India, there is something to grab your attention.

The delegation of which I was a part was armed mainly with a $50 million war chest that we were authorized to spend buying whatever equipment the Indian military needed to wage war on the rooftop of the world. More specifically, we were supporting six Indian Mountain Divisions active in Ladakh. Officially, I was communications planner and assistant infantry advisor. As a practical matter, we did not have enough manpower to go around to all the duties, so we had to improvise. We were ably led by Major General Jack Kelly, U.S. Army, who was in charge of the overall mission. The Deputy Commander of the Joint Mission was Brigadier General Bromitts, U.S.A.F.

Spending all that money was a major headache. Back in 1963, $50 million was a lot of money even in military terms, and it is no simple thing to spend $50 million wisely. We were deluged with U.S. contractors trying to sell us stuff for the Indian army—much of it stuff for which the Indian army had no practical use. As I said, the Indian military was many years behind us technologically, both in terms of weapons and communications systems. And to learn what they really did need and could use, we had to go to the front—or close to it—to see exactly what they had and talk to the Indian officers. We learned some practical things about the effect of intensely cold high altitude weather on weapons and machines. For example, the D-8 bulldozers had to have a super charger on them to get them started. And the steel base plates of heavy duty mortars tended to crack when the weapons were fired. We dutifully relayed useful information like this back to the Pentagon where it no doubt got filed away somewhere.

I spent a lot of time traveling to and fro and schmoozing with my counterparts in the Indian military. The good thing was that although India is a chaos of several hundred languages and dialects, almost everyone we dealt with spoke clear English—a legacy of the long British influence in India. I think it fair to say that the English language makes a unified India possible.

We lived in the U.S. Embassy compound in New Delhi when we first arrived, but apparently the diplomats were uncomfortable having all that military brass around. Within a few weeks, they had us lodged in an apartment complex in the outer suburbs. It actually proved to be quite accommodating and livable. We each had our own little apartment and a private shower and bath. Not big, but private. The Indian family living upstairs took care of our laundry, more or less. They managed to burn an impression of an iron in one of my new suits, but I let it slide. They heated their irons on the stove and had trouble controlling the temperature. They were seriously poor people. As we got to know them, we created a pool of money intended to enable their kids to attend school. I can only take it on faith that the money was spent for that. They were from one of the lower castes—I could never keep them all straight—that still characterized Indian life in those days. Being from the U.S., and from a southern state, I was of course familiar with racial prejudice, but it did not impress me any more favorably in India than it did in my own country. Senseless racist attitudes wreak terrible havoc on human beings to no valid purpose whatsoever.

The Indian army's communications were primitive to say the least. They were using high frequency radios for most routine communication, and you cannot put a lot of traffic on HF radios. The band is too small and of course their signals will not effectively traverse high mountains. But neither could we rely on standard wires for much of our communication because the environment up north was so harsh. Much of the time, the poles and wires were under snow. Of course, the moisture of the snow will always do quick work on the steel wires. It was worse than Korea in terms of the weather and the hilly terrain. And for whatever reasons they had no carrier pigeons. For better or worse, mostly worse, the Indians had to rely on the HF radios.

The good news is that most of the shooting was done by the

time we arrived on the scene. There were still some incidents of hostile fire, and both sides kept losing combat soldiers to the ice and snow, but the governments of China and India were content to back off and were haggling over a settlement. The negotiations dragged on for months, however, and we had no way of knowing when a formal end to the hostilities would be announced. Our experience in Korea had taught us to never take anything for granted where communist governments were involved. In the meantime we kept doing what we could to support the Indian Mountain Divisions.

I made some interesting friendships among Indian officers, many of whom had trained at Sandhurst in Great Britain, or at least acquired some training there. They, of course, spoke impeccable English, perhaps a bit better than my own. More than a few of them had studied in the U.S., including Leavenworth and the Army War College. I recall with special fondness one Indian brigadier general who invited me to play golf. There is no quicker way to acquire my friendship than to invite me out on a golf course, and they had some nice courses in India. I was junior to him of course, but he was clearly interested in making connections with the U.S. military at whatever level was available. I recall I encountered him up in the Himalayas where we were hooking up communications wires and doing what we could do to help. He said to me, pointing down in the valley below us, "Oh Mac, look, isn't that gorgeous?" It was in fact a beautiful landscape but he was talking about the sight of big Air Force C-130s flying in with supplies for his soldiers. I said, "Yes, that is beautiful," thinking to myself, "in more ways than you can realize."

The Indian officers were dedicated to their country and government, and competent enough, but they had a casual approach to their missions that I assumed was somehow related to their British orientation, because the British officers there on the ground also were exceedingly casual by our standards. They took hours for lunch and always broke for afternoon tea while their American counterparts, like me, were thrashing around, running to and fro and burning the midnight oil.

It was all part of the rich and various Indian landscape around me. I was fascinated by things that happened every day and by the people I met and worked with. The people of Ladakh wore funny looking hats with something that looked like horns. They kept yaks instead of cattle and used spinning wheels to make cloth. Being there among them was like going back in time. A number of stories sprang up about the effect those cargo planes had on the residents of Ladakh who had little knowledge of the outside world and had never come into contact with modern technology. One had a local insisting that when the first plane had landed in Ladakh, they brought hay to feed it. Another story had a local father watching them unload Jeeps from a plane and telling his son that when the Jeeps grew up, they would sprout wings and fly like their mother.

Not surprisingly, during this joint military-diplomatic mission, I was called upon to spend a good bit of time at the U.S. Embassy which was a fun place to be—just one reception after another replete with good food and excellent spirits. I had to go, attendance was mandatory. It was a beautiful embassy that looked a bit like the Kennedy Center in Washington, and it had a moat around it for some reason. The receptions were invariably comical. Someone always had a bit too much to drink and said or did silly things. I remember one particularly tall guy who was so eager to meet the ambassador that he did not notice a reflecting pool in his way and stepped into it. Fortunately, it was only a foot or two deep.

Everyone who was anyone in New Delhi came to these shindigs, in large part because the U.S. Ambassador to India was the legendary John Kenneth Galbraith. Appointed by President

Kennedy, Galbraith was arguably the most famous and influential American intellectual of that period—the 1950s through the 1970s. He was an unapologetic liberal and an outspoken economist, probably the best known economist in the world. He had written many books with ponderous titles like "American Capitalism" and "The New Industrial State." He taught at Harvard—of course—and was active in Democratic Party politics. He served in various positions in the administrations of Presidents Franklin Roosevelt, Harry Truman, Kennedy and Lyndon Johnson. He was one of the very few people to be awarded the Prestigious Medal of Freedom twice, in 1946 and 2000, for his contributions to economics.

Galbraith's standing was such that he routinely bypassed the Department of State hierarchy to report directly to President Kennedy. He was very close to Nehru and advised the Indian government on economic matters. He was, in other words, a very big man in New Delhi and there I was, a lowly U.S. Army captain,[5] bending his ear almost every day I was in town. I would spend two to three hours with him at a stretch, briefing him on what we had seen and done on our most recent visit to the war zones.

Actually, he was the one doing the bending. Galbraith was tall, well over six feet tall, and lanky like a basketball player. When he spoke confidentially to me, I stood up as high as I could, but he still had to bend over to talk to me. But bend he did, because I was going out in the country on a regular basis, interacting with the Indian military, dealing with the support we were bringing, and he wanted to know everything about it. I was a bit shocked by his informality at times, but soon became accustomed to working with him. He was easy going and unpretentious. He had the ear of Kennedy and Nehru, and was very influ-

---

[5] I went to India as a captain and returned as a major. General Kelly promoted me. The guy who replaced me was a major, yet another example of how I was forever performing work above my rank.

ential. It did occur to me that my words were being forwarded in one way or another to two of the most influential leaders in the free world. I grew to like Galbraith a lot and held him in high regard. Would that we could always send people of such stature to represent our country abroad.

Throughout 1963, as we gradually spent the $50 million, the war between China and India petered out. In truth, I don't believe it was ever a big deal for either side, and I never really felt in danger. The Indians, then and now, regarded Pakistan as the real enemy. If there was one significant result of the Chinese conflict, it was to prod India into upgrading its military because its weaknesses had been conspicuous. In October, I rotated back to the U.S. to my next assignment at Fort Riley, Kansas. I had been in India for about 10 months. I enjoyed my exposure to a rich and varied culture, but was glad to get back on American soil. I had left a captain and returned a major, and I was soon back with my wife and daughters.

CHAPTER 7

Moving The Big Red One

*When I first went into the active army, you could tell someone
to move a chair across the room—now you have to tell him why.*
—Maj. Robert Lembke

WHEN I WAS GETTING READY TO RETURN FROM INDIA IN 1963,
a good friend of mine in personnel took me under his wing and
advised me about my next career move. "Mac, you need to get
your career back on track," he said. "You are screwed up if you
don't get back into a tactical unit, and I can help you do that."

I knew he was right. Diplomatic ventures like I had in India
were all well and good, but for an Army officer who aspires to be
a general officer, I needed to reinforce my combat bona fides
that I had first acquired in Korea. As soon as I hit the states, I
went to El Paso to retrieve my family and we set out for Fort
Riley, Kansas, where I would join the First Infantry Division—
the famous Big Red One—which was being prepared for assignment to Vietnam where things were getting hot.

The Big Red One, so-called because of the large red numer-
al one that its personnel wear on their shoulders, was created in
1917. It is the oldest and arguably the most distinguished division in the U.S. Army. It won praise for its performance in
World War I at Soissons, St. Mihiel and the Ardennes. It was the
first division to cross the Rhine River in that war and altogether

rang up more than 22,000 casualties by the time of Germany's surrender in November 1918. In World War II, the Big Red One performed superbly in North Africa and Sicily, and on D-Day was one of two U.S. divisions to hit Omaha Beach. It was engaged through most of the fighting in Europe, helping fend off the German onslaught in the Battle of the Bulge, and leading the invasion of the German homeland from the captured bridge at Remagen. It was and remains one of our country's premier fighting units. I was honored to get that assignment.

Probably the most famous commander of The Big Red One was General Terry De la Mesa Allen who led the Big Red One into North Africa and later Sicily. He was a true soldier's soldier in the finest sense of the term. As war correspondent Ernie Pyle would later write, "Major General Terry Allen was one of my favorite people. Partly because he didn't give a damn for hell or high water; partly because he was more colorful than most; and partly because he was the only general outside the Air Forces I could call by his first name. If there was one thing in the world Allen lived and breathed for, it was to fight. He had been all shot up in the last war, and he seemed not the least averse to getting shot up again. This was no intellectual war with him. He hated Germans and Italians like vermin."

Allen's extraordinary career was all the more remarkable because he had actually flunked out of West Point. He later got his college degree from Catholic University in Washington, D.C., and then passed a competitive exam to become an Army officer. He served with distinction in both WWI and WWII. His son, who was later killed in Vietnam, was in my class at the Point.

It was a long drive from El Paso to Fort Riley, and I recall vividly listening to the terrible reports on the radio of the assassination of President Kennedy, and all of the subsequent events of those dark days. In that year, Lynn was 10 years old and

Marsha was 8, so they were old enough to have some understanding of what was happening. It was a sobering time for us, as it was for everyone. Of course, we had no way of knowing then what a turbulent era the 1960s would be in many ways.

We were driving a 1959 Chevrolet that I had bought when I got off the boat returning from Europe after my first assignment there. I had a preference for Chevrolets that I had inherited from my father, but that one proved to be something of a lemon and helped me become interested in other models. That was well before the Japanese car invasion had taken root, with its emphasis on quality. Detroit had yet to discover quality.

I came to Fort Riley mainly to put my boots on again and get back with active troops in the field. I was S-3 Operations Officer for a few weeks when I first got there before assuming my regular duty as executive officer for the 121st Signal Battalion. We were getting the Big Red One ready for service in Vietnam and that was no small undertaking. A division in those days consisted of between 15,000 and 18,000 personnel. The Signal Battalion had between 600-700 people. Of course, the division came equipped with tanks, personnel carriers, Jeeps, helicopters, artillery, medical units, fuel tankers, Military Police units, all of the accouterments of a modern fighting division. We were supposed to transport the whole shebang by air and put it on the ground ready to fight almost immediately.

This was before the era of the volunteer army, so most of the enlisted personnel in The Big Red One were draftees, while the officers were almost all volunteers who had gone through West Point, ROTC or OCS. They were largely garrison soldiers in the peacetime army, and one of our most difficult tasks was to make it clear they were going in harm's way and better start thinking like soldiers if they did not want to get their butts shot off.

I should interject here that this was toward the end of the brief heyday of the so-called "Pentomic" organization of the

Army that had begun under President Eisenhower and continued into the early 1960s. It was all an outgrowth of the Cold War and the presumption that our next major conflict, if one came, would be against the Soviet Union and would likely involved an exchange of nuclear weapons. It entailed reorganizing divisions into five battle groups (replacing regiments and battalions), each commanded by a colonel which could in theory be widely dispersed on a nuclear battlefield for force protection, and then rapidly concentrated for offensive action. The 101st Airborne was the first Pentomic division.

The Pentomic arrangement also made it more difficult to coordinate communications, a task that was more than complicated enough given the technology we were working with in those days, much of which was left over from Korea or even WWII. The Army had been starved for resources for a long time after the Korean War, and we were only then beginning to make up for that neglect. We were doing a good bit of research and development, but had little inventory to work with. To make matters worse, much of our equipment was not interoperable. We had different generations of communications equipment between active units and reserves that were not compatible.

Fortunately, by the time I got to The Big Red One, the Army had given up on the Pentomic system, at least as far as that division was concerned, and instead was shifting to what we called a ROAD Division[6] with Three Brigades.

Our purpose was to determine if the Big Red One could be moved by air and, if not, how much of it could be moved by air. The Air Force was feeling its oats and contended it could move the division all by itself. So we set out to determine if that were true. One of our first tasks was to lay all of the components of this division, equipment and personnel out on the ground so the Air Force brass could get a good look at what a full division con-

---

[6] Reorganization Of Army Division (ROAD)

sisted of and some idea of the challenge of moving it. So we spread it all out on the ground. It extended for over two miles. It was winter, the vehicles were running. Exhaust fumes created clouds. It must have looked like the evacuation of Dunkirk from the air. General Curtis LeMay of WWII fame was Chief of Staff for the Air Force at that time and came to watch the first exercise. I was standing to the rear of General Paul D. Adams, the four star commander of all contingency Army forces in the U.S. (CONUS). (I was serving as temporary aide to General Adams while he was at Fort Riley.) Adams was standing next to LeMay. He leaned over to LeMay and said, "Okay Curt, that's a division, haul it!" I do believe LeMay almost swallowed his cigar.

We moved the division, or at least parts of it, altogether four times during the 15 months I was there. Our first three moves were from Fort Riley to an empty swampy area near Tampa, Florida. The fourth and last one was to Missouri. I really earned my spurs in the Army through those airlifts beginning in the planning stages when I, despite my humble status as a major, challenged some of the senior officers on their plans. I would say, for example, that a certain plan was not feasible because they would end up with the division rear in front of the major control post. I insisted they had to move the communications equipment back further. As a rule, generals and colonels do not care to be corrected by majors, but in this case they could see that I was right, and they made changes accordingly.

Back in those days, our largest cargo aircraft were the C-124s. They were too big to land at the airport at Fort Riley so we had to land them at Fort Shilling Air Force Base which was about two or three hours away from Fort Riley by highway. (They were rather puny compared to the behemoths of today, but they seemed big to me then.) The upshot of all this moving about was the realization that the Air Force, at least in those days, could not move all of the components of a heavy ROAD division like the Big Red one. It was just too much to handle. When the Big Red One went to Vietnam, a lot of the heavy equipment had to go by sea.

All of which kept me busy. An Army division—really, any military unit—simply must have communications. A commander who cannot communicate with his troops might as well be sitting at his desk watching TV. We had the VRC-12 family of HF radios. We called it a family because they had overlapping bands in which the infantry could talk to the artillery or the artillery could talk to headquarters. Different units had different bands. Major portions of the band were for the exclusive use of the infantry. But then as now, there was finite amount of bandwidth to be used. Once that is used, there is no more available.

My challenge was to be able to hook up communications on the move from Fort Riley to wherever we were going. As you move military units around on tactical exercises, you first set up communications posts at division headquarters, and then put them in contact with the brigades and keep them hooked up through all sorts of weather. Once we had the links established and the trucks in place, we had communications via tactical short range radios.

We were largely dependent on what we called RATT rigs, which was short for radio teletypes, that could ride on HF signals that we were bouncing off the ionosphere. The antennas to support that are of necessity quite large. When you get to where you're going and set up shop, you have to put out these long wires that extend several meters in different directions. We took along 100 kilowatt generators on trailers to provide the juice.

We did not have much communications overlap with the Air Force, so we often had to borrow radios from them. They had air-ground liaison teams on the ground with the infantry. We would tie it all together at what we called a Tactical Operations Center (TOC) for the division. Normally, in a stable combat situation, the TOC will be 3-7 miles behind the combat area. But if the situation is fluid and you are on the move, you will optimally be in the middle of the division, with the combat units ahead and the support vehicles behind.

I got creative along the way offering innovations here and there, thanks to all the advanced education and experience I had obtained in my different postings. I was using local water towers to bounce our communications signals, a technique not in our tactical manuals, but I thought—well, why not. That's the thing about military communications—you have to be able to improvise. Young officers who come out of West Point determined to do things by the book are in for a rude awakening. You need a flexible approach to deal with a world that does not always go by the book.

On the first move from Fort Riley to Florida, I was under the nominal command of a lieutenant colonel whose background was not in communications, and who did not seem to have much grasp of the challenge before us. When we returned to Fort Riley from that first move, the division commander, a two star named Jack Seamens, called me in and said he was impressed with my performance. He said that from then on, I would be responsible for the 121st Signal Battalion. I interrupted to insist I would never undercut my boss, which is the kind of thing that will come back to haunt you. He told me not to worry, that my boss would be assigned to different duties. Seamens was in fact acting on the recommendation of his one star, Brigadier General Randy Dickens. Both West Pointers, Seamen and Dickens had decided I had a future and were determined to boost my career. Dickens in fact was a mentor who started me on my quest for a general's star. He told me I had all the qualities it took to be a general officer in that I did not think in linear terms, but rather saw the whole picture. I replied that I did not know about that, but that we definitely had people out front who should have been in the rear.

In fact, the lieutenant colonel above me who I unwittingly usurped was a very capable officer within the sphere of his specialty, which was intelligence gathering and analysis with the Army Security Agency (ASA). The ASA, which dated back to WWII, monitored enemy communications networks and tried to jam them. It was in fact the forerunner of the National Security Agency (NSA). The people who comprise agencies like that are very intelligent, as was that young officer, but have a different mindset from people like me on the firing line. That lieutenant colonel went on to a fine career at the ASA, and nothing negative attached itself to my name for assuming responsibility for the Signal Battalion.

And I, once again, found myself exercising responsibility above my rank, which was becoming a career habit. But I was in my element on those mobilizations, anticipating problems, setting up communications and making sure the senior officers could communicate with subordinates throughout the operations. They appreciated that and my career progressed accordingly.

During my time with The Big Red One, I received a high accolade from the division's Operations Officer Lt. Col. Miles Vaughn, who was impressed with my ability to overcome challenges. "McKnight," he said, "I do believe you could communicate out of hell." Several people overheard that comment, and I would hear it repeated many times more over the years. Vaughn was a fine officer and a good friend, so it meant all the more coming from him.

I had one fairly hairy experience during one of the transfers to Florida. I was riding on a C-130 with some of our communications vehicles that were strapped down with chains to prevent them from moving during transport. The pilot came down on a tactical runway that was really nothing more than a mud strip. It was like hitting Velcro. The aircraft just stopped in its tracks.

The trucks went down on their springs and popped up, breaking many of the chains holding them in place. The cargo shifted and I was pinned against the fuselage by a Jeep. The pilot came back and helped free me. We were both majors. He said he was not going to move that aircraft again, that God only grants us so many passes in this life and he had just used his up. I do not believe I was seriously injured, though I have had stiffness in my neck since that day. But it is a fact of life that anytime you move an Army division from one place to another, people get hurt, sometimes fatally. That is the way of the world. It is what it is.

During my time at Fort Riley, I scarcely saw Barbara or the girls, which I regret. There was so much to do and all the moves meant I was in transit much of the time. But they adapted well, as they always did. "I remember Ft. Riley fairly well," said Lynn. "On the weekends, Marsha and I would often walk to the craft shop where we made ceramic items like ashtrays and egg cups, which we would eventually bring home to Mom and Dad. Life on post was very sheltered. We walked everywhere by ourselves and played outside until dark. The post itself was beautiful, having been planted with flowers and fruit trees during WWII by prisoners housed at Ft. Riley. Marsha and I were very involved with the Girl Scouts and Mom was our scout leader. We sang in the junior choir at the post chapel. I got to go to the post stables with a friend to ride her horse. Ft. Riley has a significant history with the cavalry and the last living cavalry horse, named Chief, had been stabled there. I also remember taking square dance lessons. I attended half of 5th grade and all of 6th grade at the elementary school on post."

All during this time, I was working diligently to master my craft to a higher level under the presumption I would be going with The Big Red One to Vietnam. I had really committed to it. In fact, I rarely saw Barbara and the girls during this time, though we were ostensibly living in the same quarters. I was forever off with the division on maneuvers. Certainly, Seamens and Dickens were also operating under that assumption that I would accompany them to Vietnam. I had done well moving the division around and there was, after all, a war on.

But the Army works in marvelous ways its wonders to perfect. One day out of the blue I received orders from Washington to uproot my family once again, only this time my destination was not Vietnam—it was El Salvador. Some great planner in Washington had apparently pulled my name out of a hat or something. "You can't fight what Washington wants you to do," said General Dickens. "You have done a marvelous job getting this division ready for combat, but obviously this is an important job they want you to do in El Salvador."

But first I had some more training to undergo, and also had to brush up on my language skills. I was sent to Leavenworth for a while, which I was able to handle commuting back and forth to Fort Riley on weekends, and then I was sent on to Fort Ord in California for advanced lessons in Spanish.

Our time at Fort Riley was rich in childhood experiences for Lynn and Marsha who were coming of age, making friends and learning games and crafts. They went to the movies on Saturdays, and often we dined out at a Chinese restaurant. All of that began to wind down when I began my studies at Leavenworth. "Mom was really a trooper during the time Dad was commuting back and forth to Fort Leavenworth," Marsha recalled. "I knew it was tough for her to say goodbye to him every Sunday. But as usual, she kept our lives humming and as normal as possible during his absence."

My family came with me to Fort Ord, and later on to El Salvador. The language school was demanding, in part because I would be expected to teach English to Spanish speaking El Salvadorans. Of course, Spanish is a language of immense variety. They gave us a different instructor at different times of the day-a Cuban, then a Mexican, then a Puerto Rican, then a Venezuelan. The purpose was to convey the music of the language more than specific grammar that can vary from country to country.

We were only in Fort Ord for four months, but we put the girls in school as soon as we got there. "When Dad came home and told us we would be moving to El Salvador after a few months in California, I cried," said Lynn. "I didn't know where El Salvador was. We got out the encyclopedia and studied the article and maps of the country. At the end of 6th grade, we moved to Fort Ord. Although Marsha and I had finished school in Kansas, Mom enrolled us in school for the last two weeks of school in California as their schools were still in session. We were not thrilled, but we did get to meet some people before summer started."

To the extent my military career has been successful, I owe much of that success to the resourceful women in my family. It was never easy for them bouncing from one country to another, but they made the most of it, and indeed prospered by learning much about the world and their own ability to overcome obstacles. And soon we were off to Central America.

I was class honor senior at Whitehaven High School in Memphis, Tennesee. I was also "Mr. Whitehaven."

High frequency radio operator in the 1930s between the wars.

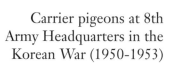

Carrier pigeons at 8th Army Headquarters in the Korean War (1950-1953)

With Barbara receiving CINC South Award Joint Commendation Medal from Gen. George R. Mather in Panama Canal Zone in 1969.

PHILCO *transac* S-2000

WORLD'S FASTEST ALL-TRANSISTOR DATA PROCESSING SYSTEM

GREATER VALUE FOR YOUR COMPUTATION DOLLAR

The Philco 2000 at White Sands Missile Signal Support Agency, White Sands, New Mexico.

Me as Commanding General of the 5th Signal Command in Worms, West Germany, in 1979. (Reforger Exercise)

World War II
Recruiting Poster.

VRC-12 Radio (1960)

Tropospheric Scatter Dish.

Signal Corps unit
making a movie

A Patch Panel Communication Van.

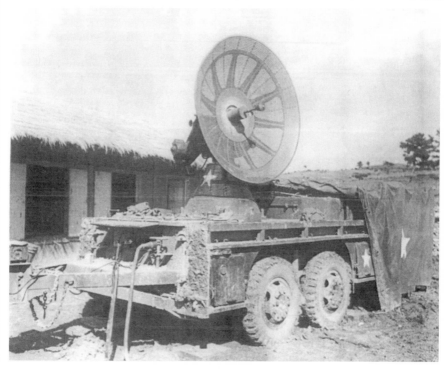

Long Range Radio Signaling Vehicle

Soldier with a cumbersome radio telephone VRC-74 (Vietnam).

Presenting a joke gift to departing Major General Robert Tabor.

Col. Mc Knight is shown here as he blasts out of the sand pit during the Inter-Staff Golf Tournament for USACC.

A moment in history: History was made when we had six Three Star Generals in the Signal Corp. Left to right: Don Rodgers, Emmett Paige, V. O. Lange, Robert Donahue, James Rockwell, Clarence McKnight

Smart phones with U.S. Army (aps) in Afghanistan in 2012.

Mobile computing command control systems on the move in Afghanistan in 2012.

THE WHITE HOUSE

WASHINGTON

April 9, 1987

Dear General McKnight:

On the occasion of your retirement from
the United States Army after 35 years of
professional service, I want to express my
congratulations and my deepest appreciation
for the loyal and faithful service you have
given our Nation. Few people have the
satisfaction of rising to the top of their
profession, and even fewer have demonstrated
the vision and leadership you have shown as
we move into the Information Age. Your dedication and untiring efforts to improve the
reliability and capabilities of our worldwide
military communications systems have been a
major factor in our national security posture.

Nancy joins me in wishing you a fulfilling
retirement, and we're confident you will
keep making contributions to the life of
our Nation in years to come. God bless you.

Sincerely,

Ronald Reagan

Lieutenant General C. E. McKnight, Jr., USA
Director for Command, Control
    and Communications Systems
Joint Chiefs of Staff
Washington, D.C. 20301-5000

CHAPTER 8

Central America

*In the field of world policy, I would dedicate this nation
to the policy of the good neighbor.*
—President Franklin D. Roosevelt

OUR NATION'S RELATIONSHIP WITH THE COUNTRIES OF CENTRAL
and South America has long been a sore point with critics of
American foreign policy. Historically, the nations of Central
America in particular have never been a top priority of
Washington. They were small countries—Costa Rica, El
Salvador, Guatemala, Costa Rica, Nicaragua, and Panama—
characterized by marginal economies, rampant poverty and little
importance in world affairs.

In the early 1900, we often employed troops to support
repressive regimes in the region—the so-called "banana wars."
It appeared to outsiders that our primary concern was protecting U.S. business interests in Central America, not helping the
people improve their condition, and that was probably accurate.
In the 1930s, President Roosevelt made a genuine effort to atone
for that legacy of indifference, but of course his administration
was caught up in The Great Depression and then World War II.
Its overtures to Central America were exceedingly modest and
did not make much of an impression on the peoples there.

It fell to a later Democratic President, John F. Kennedy, to
breathe new life into that initiative, with his Alliance for

Progress. In 1961, President Kennedy proposed a 10-year plan for Latin America ..."to complete the revolution of the Americas, to build a hemisphere where all men can hope for a suitable standard of living and all can live out their lives in dignity and freedom." Among Kennedy's goals were an annual 2.5 increase in per capita income, establishment of democratic governments, elimination of adult illiteracy, price stability to avoid inflation or deflation, more equitable income distribution, land reform and economic and social planning. Latin America countries were to pony up $80 billion for this campaign while the U.S. forked over $20 billion.

President Kennedy, of course, was assassinated in 1963, but the Alliance for Progress continued, possibly with some added energy because of his tragic and untimely death. By 1965, I learned that an assignment to El Salvador lay in my future, possibly because my substantive experience in India identified me as an up and coming young officer who could handle foreign assignments. At the time, I was fretting that I had not yet been sent for advanced training at Fort Leavenworth, one of the mandatory road markers young officers must pass. As a major with seniority, I was overdue for that. So I finally was posted to Leavenworth in the summer of 1965, and from there was sent on to Fort Ord in California to study Spanish.

I already had a good background in Spanish, having studied it in high school and at West Point. But in El Salvador I would be expected, among other things, to actually teach in Spanish so I had to hone my skills considerably. By December of '65, Barbara and I were off with the girls for what would be a fascinating two-year tour in El Salvador, to be followed by a shorter stint in Panama. By then Lynn was approaching her teens, and Marsha was two years younger. They were bright, smart and curious, and we had no doubt they would benefit greatly from the experience. There is always some difficulty adjusting to a foreign environment, but overall El Salvador was a net positive for our family. Years later, we would all recall it with fondness.

El Salvador

El Salvador is on the bottom left of Central America, abutting Guatemala and Honduras, on the Pacific Ocean. It is a tiny country embracing only 8,169 square miles, with a maximum length of 160 miles and an average width of 60 miles. It has a good deep water port and a good road network. It has a lot of people—the densest population in the region outside Haiti. There are about 6 million people living there today. When we arrived there in 1965 it was about half that.

When we first landed, we took up residence in a motel for a month or so, The Patio Motel, before we found housing with a community of ex-pats. Lynn and Marsha were enrolled in a school that taught in both English and Spanish. I had trouble adjusting to the diet down there which is abounds in "hot" food, but got used to it after a while. (Not so much that I am inclined to order it in restaurants.)

Of course, El Salvador is a desperately poor country and there was a problem with burglars. We had two maids and a dog, with at least one on duty all the time, otherwise they would steal the windows off your house.

All told, there were about 100 military personnel in a joint Army-Air Force mission. As a Signal Corps officer, my primary task was to help the Salvadorans with telecommunications. I ended up focusing on helping them build up an electronics industry, or at least I gave it my best shot. In the U.S., we have always been heavily dependent on the private sector to provide advanced electronics, but with no infrastructure the Salvadorans had little to build upon. And as I discovered, the equipment we had was of little use to them because there was almost nothing to connect it to.

I soon realized I was more on a diplomatic mission than a military one. At that time, El Salvador's tiny military had little to do. It was very top heavy with lots of colonels and not many captains. In the years ahead, the Salvadoran army would become heavily engaged in a bloody domestic revolution that would wreak havoc throughout the country, but that lay in the future. That is not to suggest it was all sweetness and light where we were. Not everyone appreciated our presence. The year after we left, two senior U.S. military officials, Army Colonel John D. Webber, Jr., and Navy Lt. Commander Ernest A. Munro, were gunned down by terrorists in next door Guatemala. That event presaged a long social upheaval ahead that still hasn't worked itself out everywhere in Central America.

But I regarded my time there as something of a milk run. It was in the aggregate a wonderful learning experience. I spent a lot of time traveling, soaking up the countryside, getting to know the people. The climate was wonderful, at least in the northern part of the country where we were. Down along the Pacific Coast, it gets really hot and humid. They have one short monsoon season every year, after which the climate is benign, at least by my standards. The Salvadorans are generally solid family people with strong religious values. They consider themselves Americans just like us because El Salvador is, after all, in America. It was hard to argue with that. They really admired President Kennedy, who of course was dead by then. On the recommendation of a friend, I took along a supply of Kennedy half dollars that I gave away as keepsakes, a most popular gift that opened many doors for me.

I had an excellent rapport with the U.S. Ambassador to El Salvador, Raul Castro, who thought I was hot stuff. He told the State Department team that they should do what I was doing—get out and see the country and meet the people. I would pass along information to him about what I learned on my forays into the countryside. I was issued a card that said I was the ranking major in the El Salvadoran army. In earlier days, an officer in my position could draw additional pay from the host country, but by the time I arrived the Army had cut that off.

I learned that El Salvador was controlled by an oligarchy of 13 families, which was a key factor in the troubles that lay ahead. There weren't many career options available to young Salvadorans, but one was with the army, as small as it was. We tried to cultivate the best and brightest, and sent many of them to schools in the U.S. Some of our stateside critics complained we were training killers, but we were really trying to put our best foot forward down there, opening doors for people and helping them build a stronger economy and society. We were engaged in nation building at a time when Fidel Castro was building up Cuba as a communist bulwark in the Western Hemisphere and Che Guevara was fomenting revolution in South America. (Guevara was finally killed in Bolivia in 1967.) We were not carrying out military operations and were certainly not trying to kill anyone. But there was widespread insurgency through Central and South America, which was why we were there. It was an application of what I call "soft power," using our military resources to help another nation and thereby strengthen our own position while propagating democratic values.

It may seem like ancient history now, but back then we were caught up in the Cold War, and it was serious business. The Soviet Union was vying with us for world domination. It seemed like every month or two another country on the world map was being painted red. More than a few people in our own country believed socialism was the wave of the future, and that we might as well become part of it. Of course, the struggle in Vietnam was a critical phase of that great confrontation. Many people in Washington were concerned that countries in our own sphere of influence, like El Salvador, could be subverted by communist agitators.

I learned a lot about being a defense attaché type in El

Salvador, although someone else had that title. I was telecommunications advisor. I would visit the barracks of Salvadoran soldiers, bring along my radios and other equipment, and then would hang around a couple of hours teaching them English. Most of the officers I worked with seemed to have a fairly decent income, or at least they lived pretty well. I spent a good bit of time teaching them English. In training in California, I focused on translating English into Spanish. In El Salvador, using the same text books, it did it the other way. They were attentive students and listened very carefully when I spoke about my country and life in the U.S. I do believe every junior officer there had visions of being the George Washington of El Salvador. Despite that ruling oligarchy of 13 families, I sensed a strong patriotic spirit. Over the years, despite their domestic troubles, El Salvador has been a good friend of the U.S., and many Salvadorans have immigrated here.

Our wireless radios were a revelation to most rank and file Salvadorans, most of whom lived in poverty close to the land. They did not have radios and TVs in their homes, at least not back in those days. Most of the people who used radio down there were in the police department. The Salvadoran army was mainly a training unit, not fighting any wars at that time. They had an occasional border skirmish with Guatemala that never amounted to much. Most of the time those things lasted a day or so.

I was chomping at the bit for an assignment to South Vietnam where the war was heating up. Looking back, I suppose I was one of the few people eager to get there, but then I was a young Army officer and that's where the action was. But I developed a bad case of hepatitis and was deemed unfit at the time for combat duty. In truth I was really sick and almost died, or at least I felt like I was about to die. They put me in a Salvadoran hospital because I was too weak to be moved. But the good Lord took pity on me and I gradually recovered.

This was the summer of 1967. We had been in El Salvador about a year and a half when they transferred me to Quarry Heights in the Panama Canal Zone. In Panama, our living quarters were equipped with air conditioning which we had not needed where we were posted in El Salvador. In the spring of '67, I was promoted to Lieutenant Colonel, right on schedule, despite my illness. I recall watching the famous World War II battleship the U.S.S. New Jersey come through the locks. It only had a few inches clearance on each side, but the canal people were pretty good at that sort of thing, and it came through okay.

My job in Panama was to validate the electronics equipment for countries in Central and South America. We had a big program called Latin American Military Communications (LAMC). I travelled all over South America—Argentina, Brazil, Chile, Venezuela and other places, in addition to the nations of Central America. This experience helped me greatly years later when I reached worldwide command. I learned a lot about the people who had founded those countries in South America. In Chile, for example, I encountered a lot of Germans who were still doing the goosestep in their military drills. I suppose some habits are hard to break. There was also a large German population in Argentina.

One night I found myself at a state dinner sitting across from Panamanian President Omar Torrijos. I was serving as translator because the regular guy could not be there, and though I was conversant in Spanish, my skills are probably not up to par by State Department standards. In any case, I remember telling Torrijos he could be the George Washington of Panama. He liked that concept, but as I recall he came up a little short.

We had some big problems with the communications down there. We were using high frequency (HF) radios, and it is very hard to channelize information on HF. It did not work very well. When I had been in Germany we had used HF to communicate back home to Andrews Air Force Base, but the topography and primitive communications infrastructure in Central and South America posed a lot of challenges that we never completely overcame.

By 1969, my health restored, I finally received orders for Vietnam. I sent Barbara and the girls back to El Paso where we had lived before. They knew a lot of people there and the girls had a lot of friends, or thought they did. All military brats have to cope with lots of moves and absent fathers much of the time. "El Paso was the worst," Lynn said. "Dad was gone. We were living off post in an apartment complex for a year. The high school we went to was in the same neighborhood we had lived in years before, and we expected to rekindle old friendships. But it did not work out that way. The kids we thought would remember us did not. It was a big high school with fraternities and sororities. It was very clickish and we did not fit in. In my junior year, I ordered a ring for a high school I knew I would not graduate from."

At this late date, it pains me to think of the terrible time that El Salvador went through in the years after we left. There was widespread social unrest. The poor people, of whom there were many, waged guerilla warfare on the propertied classes—those 13 ruling families I spoke of earlier. A militant communist insurgency led by the FMLN (Farabundo Marti National Liberation Front) undertook to destabilize the government—sabotaging bridges, cutting power lines, destroying coffee plantations, anything to undermine the economy. If there was anything that poor country did not need, it was economic sabotage. The government responded with paramilitary death squads that carried out many atrocities. By 1980, a full-fledged civil war was underway. The military wiped out entire villages suspected of harboring rebels. Some of the more outrageous acts were widely reported in the U.S. For example, Archbishop Oscar Romero was shot to death in 1980, four U.S. church workers were raped and murdered that same year, four Dutch journalists were murdered in 1982 and six Jesuit priests, along with their housekeeper and her daughter, were shot to death in 1989

The war persisted for years despite many efforts to put an end to it. The FMLN refused to participate in elections, and the government refused to participate in peace talks organized by the FMLN. Growing support of the communist government in nearby Nicaragua prompted our government to continue military aid to the El Salvadoran government, despite its atrocities. We finally cut off military aid in 1990 after the United Nations became involved.

As for Kennedy's Alliance for Progress, it never amounted to much. Kennedy's successor, President Lyndon Johnson, was too preoccupied with the war in Vietnam, and anti-war protests in the streets, and his own homegrown "Great Society" vision, to worry much about Central and South America. President Nixon later curtailed much of the aid we had been sending to the region. Even so, living standards were gradually improving, along with schools, health care and transportation infrastructure. Today, the U.S. sends about $35 to $40 million a year in aid to El Salvador. It has been a long hard road for the Salvadorans, and they have many problems, but they have not lost faith in the U.S. Many thousands of them today live in the U.S. and travel back and forth constantly. We enjoy a strong relationship with that country, despite the troubles of earlier years for which we bear some responsibility.

CHAPTER 9

Vietnam

You will kill ten of our men, and we will kill one of yours, and
in the end it will be you who tire of it.
—Ho Chi Minh

So AS A LIEUTENANT COLONEL, I FINALLY GOT MY ORDERS FOR
Vietnam in the spring of 1969 and spent the bulk of the year
there. By that time, the Vietnam War had become a lightning
rod for the country. It seemed to drag on and on, consuming
ever more people and resources, with no end in sight. Antiwar
street demonstrations became commonplace. This was something new to me and others in my profession. We had been
weaned on WWII and Korea in which support on the home
front was a given. That is not meant to suggest that the
American people enjoyed going to war, but patriotism tended to
minimize dissent. At least the military people in harm's way back
then felt they had solid support behind them.

At the time I was posted to Vietnam, I cannot say I possessed
any unique insights into what was rapidly becoming a national
nightmare. I was a professional soldier and there was a war on;
end of story. Of course, it was clear to everyone that we were
making little progress over there, but as a military officer you are
trained to close ranks, salute and go do your duty. So like many
thousands of my colleagues, I attended to my family—sending
them to El Paso—and reported for duty.

In retrospect, I believe our fundamental mistake in Vietnam—not counting the decision to go in there in the first place—was in trying to apply overwhelming military force in what was in essence a civil war in a primitive country. The primary responsibility for this decision lay not with the political leadership in Washington, but with the military leadership in Vietnam, which was driven by General William Westmoreland, a South Carolina native with a sterling record in WWII and Korea. There were more than a few people trying to explain to Westmoreland that this was a different kind of war that required a different kind of power, but Westy did not take advice. From 1964 through 1968, he orchestrated an overwhelming application of U.S. military might that just grew and grew with every passing year until we had more than half a million men on the ground, about two thirds of them Army, many more allied troops, and untold numbers of aircraft, artillery and tanks. In retrospect, it seems obvious we should have been building up the South Vietnamese army to fight its own war. Instead, Westmoreland pushed them aside and sent U.S. troops into the back country in a futile effort to come to wipe out the Viet Cong and North Vietnamese regulars.

Westmoreland had one idea and one idea only—to kill enemy soldiers until they ran out of soldiers, or at least the will to fight. Thus, began the grim body count reported on the evening news every night in which the number of enemy casualties was posted alongside the number of our casualties, like some sort of sporting match. But our enemies did not have to answer to public opinion like our leaders in Washington did. Westmoreland boasted that we were killing 10 of theirs for every one of ours. His fellow South Carolinian, Senator Ernest "Fritz" Hollings, said to him, "Westy, the American people don't care about the ten. They care about the one."

Hollings could have been talking to a fence post.

Westmoreland had his ideas of how to pursue the war and they were the only ideas he was interested in. Gradually, the political leadership began to realize Westmoreland was in over his head, but it was too late for President Johnson. By 1968, President Johnson was in retirement, and our new President Richard Nixon made it clear he intended to shut down the Vietnam venture. As fate would have it, that would take a lot longer than Nixon or anyone else anticipated. The war continued for several more bloody years, as did the street demonstrations and unspeakable damage to the morale of the U.S. Army.

In the spring of 1969, when I got there, American forces in Vietnam peaked at 543,000, after which we began a long drawdown. I was posted as the battalion commander designee of the Signal Battalion of the Ninth Division which, as fate would have it, would within months be one of the first to start going home. But decisions like that were well above my pay grade. I reported for duty to do what I was trained to do—enable commanders to communicate with their fighting units in the field.

Vietnam posed some awesome challenges to people in my line of work. The mere transmission of information to and from Vietnam was a major undertaking because there were no undersea cables reaching that remote part of the globe. The nearest trans ocean cable reached the Philippines.[7] We depended on radio using the relatively new tropospheric and ionospheric over the horizon scatter techniques mentioned earlier. These techniques reflected radio waves off the troposphere that ranges from 7 to 30 miles up, and the ionosphere that goes up 90 miles. As the term "scatter" implies, the signals are fragmented and reassembled by receivers on the ground. Both methods provided high quality signals less susceptible to jamming than ordinary radio. And unlike microwave relays, scatter communications did

---

[7] It was later connected to the U.S. Government Wet-Wash undersea cable connecting to Nrg Trang, Vietnam.

not require line of sight between stations. Tropospheric relay stations could be as much as 400 miles apart, compared to about 40 miles for microwave stations, a distinct advantage for forces operating in hostile territory.

Of more direct interest to me was providing tactical communications in the field. The rapid buildup of U.S. forces on the ground in Vietnam posed severe challenges to communications, as would any such buildup of military personnel, but in this case our problems were magnified because of the elimination of the post of Chief Signal Officer in 1964. That robbed the Corps of an advocate at the highest levels of the military and created disarray in the chain of command.

We did have a new combat radio, the transistorized FM model AN/PRC-25, which gave soldiers and Marines increased communications capability. It was more powerful than previous sets and provided voice communications on 920 channels and covered longer distances—three to five miles—across a wider span of frequencies. The combat troops called it the "Prick 25" which is the kind of term combat troops always employ, but they were glad to have it. A later version, the AN/PRC-77 worked even better. Their overlapping frequencies enabled the infantry, armor and artillery to talk to each other.

For the first time, the Signal Corps created an area communications system linking the chain of command into a grid that enabled it to communicate directly with each subordinate unit. Multichannel and radio relay equipment made the intricate interconnections possible. Stated another way, for the first time our combat troops no longer depended on wires to communicate. A new era of battlefield communications had arrived.

Riverine Operations

The Ninth Division had three brigades, called the Mobile

Riverine Force, in the Mekong Delta, as hostile an environment for combat as you could imagine-a densely populated, low marshy area surrounding the Mekong River. The Viet Cong were very active there, and the Ninth was constantly engaged in combat. I was commanding a platoon billeted on the U.S.S. Benewah, a troop ship moored in the Mekong River.

It was a totally different kind of war for the Army, at least based on our experience in WWII and Korea. In those conflicts, there was always a concept of a line between "us" and "them." The lines were always fluid, of course, as the fortunes of battle waxed and waned, but you learned to operate in terms of a "front" and a "rear." There were no front lines in Vietnam. The enemy was everywhere but not to be found until they wanted to be.

So we established fire bases here and there across the Vietnamese countryside, like castles in the Middle Ages, from which military units operated on search and destroy missions into the field. We established perimeters of defense around the fire bases that the enemy was forever trying to breach. We maintained 24-hour vigilance. The divisions were headquartered in the fire bases, and the brigades had smaller fire bases in surrounding areas.

In this somewhat chaotic environment, a Signal officer has to be creative and resourceful, always looking for something that works, always with a backup plan in your hip pocket. You learned to mix and match everything you had at your disposal. I have seen many bright young officers with engineering degrees fall on their faces trying to find the perfect solution. You can never find a perfect solution. I was always looking around for those "seat of the pants" sergeants and warrant officers who knew how to cut corners. You must know how to improvise. Bright young lieutenants looking for a "perfect solution" were accidents waiting to happen. Time after time, I saw them fall flat on their faces because they did not know how to improvise.

By the time I got there, the Ninth Division had adapted to its environment with classic American ingenuity. The Ninth was light but still well armed. We had helicopters, "swamp buggies," and low draft boats driven by fans like they use in the Everglades or swampy areas of the Mississippi River bayou country. The troops used these to great effect swooping in on suspected enemy redoubts. Unlike in other parts of Vietnam, the delta country, with its high water table, did not permit construction of extensive underground tunnels as were common for the Viet Cong and North Vietnamese elsewhere. When we got reports of enemy forces in the area, we ran them down and they had to stand and fight. The Ninth was nicknamed "The Old Reliables" and for good reason. They were very effective in the field, taking a heavy toll on the enemy.

My platoon's job was to keep everyone in contact with each other, which is not easy to do when they are scattered around a swampy area in helicopters and swamp buggies and air boats. I would come and go by helicopter, landing on the deck, the helipad, of the Benewah, which was a converted liberty ship, first commissioned in 1946 and later re-commissioned to serve in Vietnam in 1967. I spent a good bit of time there and must admit it was comfortable, at least compared to what the troops in the field had to put up with. I had access to good food and regular showers.

The commander of the Ninth Division was Major General Harris W. Hollis, who had come to Vietnam straight from Washington, D.C., where he had been in charge of suppressing the riots that broke out in the wake of the assassination of Dr. Martin Luther King, Jr. Interestingly, I had been caught up in that. I was posted to Central America at the time, but had come back to Washington on official business. I flew into Andrews Air Force Base in Maryland, and some bright-eyed military driver took me straight into Washington and dropped me off in the middle of a riot. A kindly black cab driver took one look at me, said "You're too white to be here," and took me over to Fort Myer on the Virginia side. I will never forget the stupidity of the first driver, or the kindness of the second.

General Hollis was a devout Christian and a wonderful guy who I recall with great fondness. Every evening at 5:00 before the officers' mess he offered a briefing of some sort, usually with people from the news media, and often with some special guests on hand, such as politicians, TV personalities or movie stars.

All of these nightly sessions also included progress reports from each of the three brigades. One night an eager young officer reported that we should prepare for the monsoons which were coming our way because the trade winds were causing havoc, or some such thing as that. General Hollis said that was an interesting report, son, and tomorrow would you be so good as to tell us some more about those trade winds. This of course was a major invitation to a young officer who the next night came armed with an arsenal of information about trade winds. When he finally concluded his extensive report, Harris said, "Thank you son, now I know a lot more about trade winds than I ever wanted to know."

That comment brought a loud laugh from the assembled officers. And though I am sure it was mortifying to that young officer who knew so much about the weather, it was the kind of thing that endeared General Hollis to his command. I was learning then, if I had not learned before, that a senior officer really must have a sense of humor to surmount that invisible barrier between him and subordinates. You need to be able to laugh even if you are the butt of the joke, and maybe especially if you are the butt of the joke. The near total absence of a sense of humor was a major failing of General Westmoreland.

I had not been in-country long, just 69 days in fact, when word came that two of the Ninth's three brigades would be rotating back to the states in part of what would become a long drawdown of U.S. forces in Vietnam. The Riverine Brigade would be the first to leave. One night General Hollis called me in. "Mac," he said, "get ahold of the mayor of Seattle, whoever it is, and tell him we want a parade when the Ninth comes back to Fort Lewis.[8] Give me an answer by tomorrow morning."

So there I was in Vietnam, the other side of the world, and I am supposed to arrange a parade for the Ninth Division in Seattle, and please do it right now, thank you very much. I thought about something my former boss General Jack Albright had told me, that you can do pretty much anything if you go through the White House. So I called on a friend who gave me a contact at the White House through whom we went to the senior communications officer at Fort Lewis who of course did know the mayor of Seattle, or at least knew how to reach him. I sweated bullets all night. Finally, about 4 a.m., I got a call from Fort Lewis that the mayor had agreed to the parade. All they needed was a formal message from us, which I assured him would be forthcoming. When I told General Hollis this, he gave me a robust pat on the back. "Mac," he said, "I heard it said that you could communicate from hell, and now I believe it."

General Albright, by the way, was one of the few senior officers I knew who took a perverse pleasure in chewing me out for both real and imagined failings. Why did you do this? Why did you do that? What's the matter with you? I complained to him about it once. He said, aw Mac, it's good for you. And I took it in good spirit because I knew he was a true friend and besides, everyone in the Army gets chewed out from time to time. It goes with the territory.

When the Riverine brigades shipped out, it was up to me to decide what communications equipment to send with them and what to keep in Vietnam. Of course, there was still a war going

---

[8] The Ninth Division was based in Fort Lewis in Washington, not far from Seattle.

on and we needed to provide the troops what they needed. But there was no way of knowing what the Ninth Division would be called upon to do next, so they had to have sufficient equipment to do their job. I had to make a lot of tough calls, some of them based on pure guesswork, but as I have said, you can never have the perfect solution.

After those two brigades shipped out, the remaining brigade, including me and my staff, was moved to Long Binh, a huge U.S. military installation about 30 miles from Saigon. It was like a little American city with some 50,000 civilian and military personnel surrounded by a well-armed perimeter. The North Vietnamese and Viet Cong had attacked it in the past, but by the time I go there it was virtually impregnable. I was with the First Signal Brigade, under command of Major General Thomas Rienzi, which was responsible for military communications in the entire peninsula. I spent the remainder of the year there.

During my time in Vietnam, like in Korea, I shot every weapon I had just to be sure I could use them if I got caught in a firefight. I always carried a .45 automatic and at times also an automatic weapon. But as in Korea, I never had to use those weapons in combat. I was most fortunate in that regard, because there was fighting all around me during those two tours of duty, and it was just random chance that I never got personally caught up in it.

But to say I never personally killed anyone does not really address the issue. I know that in doing my job right, I was responsible for killing many enemy combatants. I was involved in all of it—coordinating troop movements, calling in artillery, calling in airstrikes. I was a warrior, that was my calling and I never had a problem with it.

Germany-Second Tour

At the end of 1969, I received orders in December to move yet again—this time back to Germany. It must be remembered that during those years, we were still very much engaged in the Cold War and the main threat, as we perceived it, was the Soviet Union, and the most direct threat from the Soviet Union was an invasion of Europe. So as the Army began to downsize its commitment to Vietnam, it began moving troops and equipment back to Europe. I have heard some say that our major failing in Vietnam was in trying to fight it like we were training to fight in Europe, and there may have been some truth to that.

So in January 1970, I swooped through El Paso to pick up Barbara and the girls, and off to Germany we went. (By that time, the girls had had enough of El Paso.) Lynn was a junior in high school and Marsha was in the 10th grade. This German assignment would add up to six straight years I would be out of the country. All the moves were hard on my family, but it is a great credit to them that they dealt with it, and made the most of it. They prospered among the other military families posted there in Germany, learning to sing together in chapel, and doing well in school. I know many military "brats" have a hard time with all the moving about. To be plucked from one school and dropped into another abruptly can disrupt the education pattern. But our kids were extremely bright and surmounted the challenge. Lynn graduated from Wurzburg High School the following year—1971—as salutatorian!

"It was a Department of Defense school, and most of my classmates were dependents of military personnel," Lynn said. "It was a very welcoming environment, especially following El Paso. There were only 73 students in my graduating class. Our graduation baccalaureate was held in the Residenzplatz (Bishop's residence chapel), a gorgeous place." Lynn's salutatorian speech was entitled, "The Cultural Advantages of an Overseas Education."

During this period, Marsha developed some close friendships with a Mormon family on the base, became interested in the Mormon faith, and was eventually baptized as a Mormon. As mainline Protestants, Barbara and I were somewhat nonplused by this, but reluctant to intervene. On one occasion, a chaplain challenged me on it, wanting to know why I accepted it. I told him most of the young people I was seeing around me in those days, the children of military families, were drinking and using drugs, but that the Mormon kids were clean and straight. All things considered, I figured Marsha could be in much worse company. (When we returned stateside, and Marsha lost contact with the Mormon family in Germany, she gradually returned to our more traditional religious orientation.)

Barbara and the girls did not see much of me for the time we were in Wurzburg. Still a Lieutenant Colonel, I was commander of the 123rd Signal Company with the Third Division. The Third's commanding general, Robert Tabor, took an instant dislike to me, and said so, but I set about doing my job. Anyone who has a lot of career changes is going to encounter situations like that. You just have to do your best and hope for the best.

Most of my work related to anticipation of a possible Soviet invasion, which means I was moving more towards strategic than tactical communications. I had been engaged in purely tactical communications in Korea and Vietnam, but had focused on strategic communications in India and Central America. Even then, I was relying on my ability to see the big picture. We were constantly moving about among the European nations setting up communications systems, anticipating how to react in case of a showdown with the Soviets, and negotiating all of the twists and turns of political intrigue that characterized our military units in Europe during those unsettled years.

I was in command of about 650 people, and therein lay my biggest challenge. The U.S. Army ranks were still comprised mainly of draftees, and a substantial number of the people drafted during the Vietnam War were ill-educated, ill-tempered and ill-suited for military service. Not all of them had been to Vietnam, but the demoralization of Vietnam permeated the ranks wherever they were. Many of them were inner city minorities who brought a lot of cultural baggage with them, in addition to the racial hostility that was ubiquitous during those tumultuous years. Drug abuse, especially marijuana smoking, was epidemic. Threats against officers were commonplace. It was widely reported that officers in Vietnam who were deemed too eager for combat had been "fragged" by disgruntled troops[9]. In Germany, most of us kept loaded .45s in our desks just in case things got out of hand. I had seen some tough duty in Vietnam, but the follow-up in Germany was like an extended battle zone with dangers lurking around every corner.

I did everything I could think of to bridge the racial divide. I had worked with blacks growing up in Memphis, though I cannot recall being close friends with any one of them. As commanding officer, of course, it was a bit late to try to forge friendships with rank and file troops, but I could try to communicate. I was, after all, a communications officer. So I spent a lot of time with minority soldiers, listening to their gripes and complaints, and offering them guidance on their conduct. I haunted the barracks, even on weekends, trying to identify the drug dealers, trying to weed out the troublemakers. But I went to great lengths to treat everyone fairly. I repeated over and over that they should not squander their money on booze and prostitutes. I advised them to write to their families and to send money to their mothers. I do not know to what extent my advice was acted upon, but I did hear from various sources that I had earned the reputation of a "cool commander." I would not care to guess whether that reputation was a plus or a minus on my permanent record, but it reflected my earnest effort to bridge the gap.

---

[9] A slang term that referred to tossing a live grenade into an officer's living quarters.

I should not overstate the extent of the morale problems we had. I would say in that year I spent about 90 percent of my time dealing with issues with about two percent of our soldiers. I was constantly doing paperwork to get the drug dealers and abusers locked up. I hated to do it, but beyond a certain point, military discipline demands action.

And I will add that not all of our morale issues were generated by the ranks. Most of my fellow officers were dedicated patriots, but I heard more than a few of them snort that Vietnam was not much of a war, but "it's the only war we've got." I do not believe that kind of macho talk served us well with people in the ranks or civilian life.

I also had some West Point graduates that I would not put in as company commanders because their behavior was too erratic. I had trouble believing they had been graduated from the same West Point I attended. Everyone I served with in Korea was first rate, and I had wonderful officers in Vietnam, but some real problems in Germany. The next time I was in the U.S., I went by West Point and called upon General William Allen Knowlton, West Point superintendent, to express my concerns. I told him I had commanded three battalions, one after the other, and it almost broke me. Knowlton, a WWII vet who would later rise to a four star and serve as Military Representative to the North Atlantic Treaty Organization (NATO), told me the problem was real, but that it reflected what was going on in society at that time. When I returned to the U.S. late in 1971, I saw a headline in *The Washington Post* that said, "Army in Anguish."

By that time, I had some personal anguish of my own when I got word that my sister Dorothy Irene—there were only two of us—had perished in a tragic house fire. This hit me hard. She was a tiny woman, very smart and disciplined and a devout Christian. She got married just out of high school and had a good marriage of some 20 years, but her first husband was killed by a tornado that hit Jackson, Mississippi, where they were living in 1966 when I was in El Salvador. She remarried two years later to a widower in her church. Their house caught fire and the two of them died from smoke inhalation. In the spring of 1971, I had to take emergency family leave to come home for her funeral.

It was a tough time for me and a most difficult time for the Army because of the low morale and drug abuse. I did my best to cope with all of it, but it was a tough time all around. As I left Germany from this my second tour there, General Tabor, who had welcomed me so rudely when I came in, called me in and said he had changed his mind about me. He said he respected my commitment and determination because I never backed off. His recommendation helped me move on to my next assignment which was back in the U.S. to attend the Army War College. Tabor was later promoted to a three star and became the "Drug Czar" for the U.S. Department of Defense.

CHAPTER 10

A Turning Point

These are the times that try men's souls.
—Thomas Paine

THE U.S. ARMY EVERY YEAR SELECTS SEVERAL HUNDRED OFFI-
CERS, usually lieutenant colonels and full bird colonels, to attend
the U.S. Army War College in Carlisle, Pennsylvania. In the
autumn of 1971, I was selected for this prestigious program, and
was glad to get it, not only in terms of career advancement, but
also for a chance to return to my country for a while. Only two
from my division were chosen for this honor, which occasioned
some jealousy—perhaps resentment is the more accurate term—
among my fellow officers. In fact, the Division commander, the
same guy who had welcomed me with such open hostility, promised to make me G-1 (senior communications officer) of the
Division if I would stay. But I had my mind made up. I told him
I was the oldest lieutenant colonel in the division, and that I saw
the War College as an opportunity to advance my career. I told
him I believed I had something unique to offer the Army, and he
agreed with me. So off I went.

Founded in 1901 by Secretary of War Elihu Root, the purpose of the War College is "Not to promote war, but to preserve
peace by intelligent and adequate preparation." The War
College sits on a 500 acre campus amid a beautiful rolling countryside that seems to promote thoughtful analysis, or so it

seemed to me. It is a split-functional institution. While a great deal of emphasis is placed on research, the 600 or so students are also instructed in leadership, strategy and joint-service international operations. Today, about half the students today participate in a two-year Internet-based program, and the other half in a 10-month on-campus program. Of course, when I was there, there was no Internet program. It was a one-year course that began in late summer.

The War College brings together an interesting cross section of potential leaders including personnel from the Army (active, Reserve and National Guard); the Navy (active and Reserve); the Air Force (active, Reserve and National Guard); the Marine Corps (active and Reserve); and the Coast Guard. There is also a smattering of officers from other countries and senior civilian employees of the Federal Government—mainly the Pentagon, the State Department and the National Security Agency.

The unofficial mission of the War College, or at least one of them, is to provide advanced studies for young officers with the potential to become general officers. We were being exposed to national and strategic policies with the understanding that we might put that knowledge to effective use in senior commands in later years. In reality, only a few War College grads become general officers, but it doesn't hurt your career aspirations.

I had Barbara and Marsha with me. By that time, Lynn was off attending New Mexico State University in Las Cruces, which I suppose was an outgrowth of our time in White Sands a few years before. As I have stated elsewhere, that is an area of the country that abounds in smart people. NMSU is a top flight university. Marsha would later join Lynn there, where they both got excellent educations that have served them well over the years.

Unfortunately, while I was posted to the War College, Marsha had to attend the local high school, where there was a sharp division between civilian and military people. The "townies" routinely discriminated against the "posties." Overall, I must say the girls benefitted from their diverse school experiences, but some of the experiences were better than others.

Before reporting to the War College, I went to Memphis to look in on my mom and dad. Of course, we were all still bereaved by the tragic death of my sister a few months before. I could see it had taken a toll on my parents. I should interject here that my family had more than its share of tragedy. My grandfather, my mother's father, who managed a filling station in Memphis that included a little deli, had been murdered several years before. A cousin of mine was supposed to be on the night shift, but he had a date so my grandfather was working. It was a robbery in the middle of the night that went wrong somehow. The police suspected my father because he stood to profit from my grandfather's death. At one time my father and grandfather had been in business together, but they did not get along. In any event, I do not believe my father was involved in that killing. The police simply had no clue about what happened and so pointed the finger at my dad, but they had no evidence to support their theory and he was never charged.

I never had a close relationship with my father, probably because he was always working, or there could have been deeper reasons. He had an 11th grade education, which was actually pretty good for those days in that part of the world. In fairness, I must state that he was highly energetic and a good provider. During World War II, when there was unlimited work available, he worked three jobs. He and my mother were very much in love and had a good marriage. My visit with them this time was brief and uneventful. I had no reason to anticipate any fresh tragedies.

But a few weeks later, I was in New York with other students of the War College on a field trip to visit the United Nations. We were staying at the Roosevelt Hotel. In the middle of the night, I got a telephone call from my oldest nephew in Memphis, who was probably about 18 years old at the time. He told me my father had shot my mother who was in the hospital and not expected to live. It would be impossible to describe what was going through my mind when I got that news, and it's probably just as well. I applied for emergency leave and set out for Memphis.

The police had my father in jail. I retained a lawyer and went down to get him out. The fact that I was an Army officer I believe lent me some credibility with the authorities. The military may have been in ill repute in some parts of the country during those waning days of Vietnam, but in Tennessee my uniform still stood for something. I told them my father was under a lot of stress, had a drinking problem, and had a bad habit of playing with guns. Apparently, one night he got a bit raucous with a gun and my mother tried to take it away from him. He shot her accidentally.

So I brought my dad home, and we were going back and forth to the hospital to visit mother, who was basically on life support. She could communicate, but she could not move. It was clear to me that she was unlikely to ever regain her health. In the meantime, my father was berating me incessantly using severe language that was uncharacteristic of him. A good friend of mine who I had known since my childhood days was trying to help us and heard my dad in one of his tirades. He fetched the sheriff who came and put my father under restraint.

I found myself back in court, this time testifying against my father. I told the judge there was something wrong with him, that he was simply not himself. The court put him in a state mental hospital for evaluation. In the meantime, the police had a murder charge pending against him in case my mother died, which seemed likely. I tried to have the charge dismissed, contending he was not competent to stand trial.

On November 4, my father died suddenly of a massive heart attack. The following day, my mother died as if she knew he was gone and wanted to be with him. She was 65, he was 64. I was distraught. My mother had always been a strong, guiding force in my life. A school teacher, she was committed to academics and encouraged me to pursue higher education. I had spun my wheels for a while as a teenager, in the manner of restless teenage boys, but eventually made her proud. When my grandfather was murdered, it was she who kept the family together. She was wise and strong. She was still young with a lot of life in her when she died.

Hard Work

It would be difficult to describe my state of mind during this period, having lost my mother, father and sister all within a few months, all in tragic events that could not have been foreseen or anticipated. It is one thing to lose someone close to you after an extended illness. To lose three abruptly like that was traumatic. It was a bad year. For a while, I was depressed and despondent which was to be expected. But in retrospect, I could not have been in a better place than I was right there in Carlisle. I had my wife who has always been my rudder during times of stress. Lynn was away at college, but she and Marsha were caring and supportive.[10]

I fought the depression by focusing on my family—Barbara, Lynn and Marsha—and forced myself to think about how fortunate I truly was. And I threw myself into my work, which I have always found is a good tonic for grief. And I must say also that

---

[10] "The only way I can think that dad got through that year was through his faith in God," said Lynn. "His mother was a strong Christian woman who was always encouraging him. To this day, his morning starts with a quiet time alone, reading the Bible. Dad took Transcendental Meditation that year, and that might have helped him as well."

my fellow officers and instructors at the War College were wonderfully supportive of me during this difficult time. I cannot overstate how much that meant to me.

At the War College, I was expected to write a serious research paper of some kind to justify the government's investment in me. My superiors suggested I take on an appropriate topic like the next step in tactical communications. I demurred, suggesting instead that I address the perils of smoking marijuana which as I had just learned in Germany was a very real problem in the Army. My suggestion was accepted.

My purpose was to get into the heads of the guys who were being seduced by the drugs—marijuana and sometimes stronger things. But my primary focus was on marijuana which is a green and brown mix of dried flowers, stems, seeds and leaves from the hemp plant Cannabis sativa. The main active chemical is THC (tretrahydrocannabinol), which moves quickly through the bloodstream to the brain and other organs throughout the body. Marijuana is a mild hallucinogen that can also act as a depressant or a stimulant.

It's true that scientists have determined that the cannabis plant has the potential for addressing a range of medical conditions. But it's also true that when people are young and their bodies are still growing, marijuana actually has the potential of inflicting a long-lasting, negative impact on their brains. Using marijuana at a young age can result in structural and functional deficits of the brain. This could cause someone to develop weakened verbal and communication skills, lowered learning capabilities and a shortened attention span. Those effects were conspicuously obvious among the young soldiers using it.

In addition to the possible effects on the brain, smoking marijuana may also be hazardous to the lungs. Marijuana smoke contains 50 percent to 70 percent more carcinogenic hydrocarbons than tobacco smoke. Marijuana can be a "gateway drug" to harder drug use, and I saw more than ample evidence of that in Germany.

The War College assigned me to work on my paper with a colonel from the Military Police who shared my concerns about the impact of marijuana and other drugs on the armed forces. Our paper was published at the War College, and became a basic component of the DOD's campaign against drug abuse in later years.

When I was not focusing on the research, I embarked upon a personal quest for life's meaning. Up until that time, I had always been what you might call a "special events" Christian, observing the rituals, but not really engaged in spiritual consciousness. In my youth, we attended a Baptist Church. I essentially had the same pastor from first grade through high school. He was a wonderful man, though he was always going on about the evils of drinking and chasing women at a time in my life when I thought those things sounded pretty good. Those services lasted a long time. I recall being envious of my Catholic cousins who went to mass on Saturday night for 20 minutes and then were done for the week. But the tragic events of that year made me understand that in this life we need a spiritual anchor, a connection to the creator by whatever means we can find it.

Interestingly, I was one of two students at the War College who signed up for Transcendental Meditation. At no point did I see that as a substitute for my Christian faith, but I wanted to learn about it and derive whatever benefit I could from it. The commandant of the War College commended me for that, and put it into my permanent record. I came through that year a stronger individual and one who sees personal religious faith as a core value that we all need. I would never attempt to prescribe someone else's belief—only that every one of us needs faith. And I would never presume to say I understand the true nature of God-only that I am open to him. Sooner or later there comes a time in each of our lives when we cannot go it alone. I have always depended on friends and family, but faith is the bedrock of my life.

Turning Point

My year at The War College—1971-1972—was a turning point in my life in terms of my awareness of my mortality and consciousness of the presence of God in my life. It was also enriching for me in the way my family, friends and colleagues rallied to me in my time of crisis and helped me transcend the heartbreak. For as long as I draw breath, I will remember the flood of kindness and love what washed over me during those difficult months, and cherish the good people, living and gone, who reached out to me.

On Sunday, January 3, 1972, at the War College Memorial Chapel, I read a testimony of appreciation that I had carefully composed:

I would like to start my testimony today with a little story which was told to me by my mother when she was quite young. A small boy was playing in his room one day and decided to climb out on the roof to get a better look at the world. He climbed out of his bedroom window and sat on the sloping roof and was playing about when he suddenly started to slide down the roof. He cried out, "Please God, help me." Almost immediately, he stopped sliding. The boy gave a great sigh of relief and looked up and said, "Never mind, God. I'm hung on a nail."

Much of my early faith was like that faith of that little boy—quick to turn on and quick to turn off.

I found the church at 16, but it was more a mechanical function rather than a function of faith.

In 1953, in Korea, I learned the need of full time faith. I found that to lead troops required a 24-hour bedrock faith.

There have been great stresses in my job and in my personal life throughout the years, but the bedrock faith that I sought and found while relatively young has never let me down.

I have learned that prayer is not answered with an instant replay of the problem with a built-in easy-to-apply solution. To be a follower of Jesus Christ is to be patient and at times to suffer. Probably my most frequent prayer is, "Dear Father, please give me the strength to understand thy will."

I have witnessed large scale human sufferings in the rural south as a young boy. Later as an Army officer, I have witnessed massive human suffering and poverty in Korea, Latin America, India and Vietnam. I do not claim to understand worldwide suffering, but through faith I have obtained an inner feeling of serenity which allows me to deal with those problems which God has willed that I face as an individual.

I have felt the comfort of the nearness of God from the shores of the Mississippi River in Tennessee to the remote foothills of the Himalayan Mountains in faraway India.

Over the years my faith has turned from that of a child who was hung on a nail to that of a believer who believes that a man hung on a cross to save us, and through that man—Jesus Christ—we can be reborn and have a new, richer life which is filled with hope.

CHAPTER 11

Fort Huachuca

There is no record in history of a nation that ever
gained anything valuable by being unable to defend itself.
—*H. L. Mencken*

By THE TIME I COMPLETED MY TOUR AT THE WAR COLLEGE, I
was ready to get back to work for the Signal Corps. I had spent
much of the preceding year in reflection on the loss of my family and also on the joy of the family I still had. I had experienced
something of a spiritual awakening that would influence the
course of my life for years to come, but it was time to get back
to work. I had a career to pursue. It was 1972. The Vietnam War
was winding down, the Army was in turmoil, the Cold War was
at its height and technology was on the precipice of a new age—
though none of us fully understood that yet. We knew technology was moving ahead, but had no idea where it would go. I got
orders to report to Fort Huachuca in Arizona.

Historically, there were three major U.S. Army posts in the
United States dedicated in whole or in part to the Signal Corps:
Fort Monmouth in New Jersey that until recently was Signal
Corps headquarters; Fort Gordon in Georgia that is the site of
extensive training for Signal Corps personnel, in addition to regular combat personnel; and Fort Huachuca (pronounced wa-
chuka), in Arizona devoted mainly to research and development
and testing of new technologies. Over the course of my 35 years

in the Signal Corps, I spent a good bit of time at all three locations, but Huachuca was always my favorite.

I had visited Huachuca a few times when I was posted to White Sands missile range and found it a most inviting environment. When I got word at the War College that Huachuca was my next assignment, I was most pleased. After the tough year I had been through, a sojourn in the arid mountains of southern Arizona sounded inviting. Also, Lynn was attending New Mexico State University which was not so very far away, and we already had plans for Marsha to matriculate there as well.

Fort Huachuca dated back to 1882 when two troops of the 6th U.S. Cavalry took up permanent residence there and started erecting buildings. They were sent there to defend settlers from Native Americans of whom the fierce Apaches, led by Geronimo, were the primary threat. The fort is in Cochise County in southeastern Arizona, about 24 miles from the Mexican border. It offers a comfortable environment, away from the scorching sun of Arizona's deserts and with an ample supply of fresh water. The presence of the 6th Cavalry was reassuring to settlers and the population of the area boomed under the cavalry's protection.

In 1913, the 10th Cavalry Regiment, comprised of African Americans known as "Buffalo soldiers," was stationed there. When General John "Blackjack" Pershing led troops into Mexico chasing Pancho Villa in 1916-17, he used Huachuca as a forward supply base. In the late 1940s, the fort was closed and used by Arizona state officials as a recreation area, but by the early 50s it was reclaimed by the military as a center for electronic warfare. In 1967, it was officially designated headquarters of the U.S. Army Strategic Communications Command. However, it was becoming increasingly clear that the nature of the war in Vietnam had blurred the distinction between strategic and tactical communications, making USASTRATCOM

personnel and equipment ever more supportive of tactical operations—which is why "strategic" was dropped from the U.S.
Army Communications Command and it became officially the
U.S. Army Communications Command in 1973 when I was in
my first tour there.

The guiding light behind this transition, or at least one of
them, was General Jack Albright. I had served with General
Albright in Vietnam when he was Deputy Commanding
General of USASTRATCOM's 1st Signal Brigade, and I had
the 36th Signal Corps Area Battalion under his command. I had
the highest regard for Jack and was pleased that I would be
working for him again.

We loved Huachuca from the beginning. Barbara and the
girls thrived. Lynn was in college and Marsha, who had been
a junior in high school in Carlisle, would graduate from high
school in Arizona during this year, and join Lynn at NMSU. It
was a good time for the McKnight family, and a healing time
for me.

And I did indeed get back to work. I will offer this advice to
any and all who suffer personal losses in their lives—work is the
only viable response. There is a place for prayer, reflection and
counseling, but work is the best way to surmount heartbreak and
loss.

I had come to Fort Huachuca as a Lieutenant Colonel on the
list to become a full Colonel, and within a few weeks I had that
eagle on my shoulder. I had waited a long time for that and was
relieved to get it. That does seem to be a critical barrier to moving up the military ladder. A great many lieutenant colonels never
manage that next step, so it was a watershed in my career. Also,
my name was on the command list which meant I was eligible to
command a brigade sized unit of several thousand people when
an opportunity should appear. Things were looking up.

My job at Huachuca was that of chief of the program analysis element within the Communications Electronics Engineering and Installation Agency (CEEIA). We were responsible for Signal Corps engineering projects around the world, of which there were many. One of my superiors was Brigadier General Wes Ogden, a wonderful guy with whom I played many rounds of golf. Wes didn't have a hair on his head. We called him "Mr. Clean" after a popular commercial of that era. My immediate superior was Colonel Joe Coe, a tough veteran who had survived the Bataan death march during World War II. In those days, there were a lot of full colonels reporting to other full colonels, so there was nothing unusual about my situation.

Ogden called me in soon after I got there and gave me an assignment guaranteed to put me at odds with many of my colleagues. Apparently, I had earned a reputation going back to my first posting at Fort Monmouth for telling superiors things they did not want to hear. Ogden told me that the Signal Corps had a lot of projects afoot around the world that made little sense either in terms of need or cost. In an era of budget constraints, it was imperative that we get costs under control.

It is the nature of the military bureaucracy to conjure up expensive projects, write plans, conduct meetings, exchange memos and leave a host of projects lying around indefinitely like little bombs threatening to go off at the most inconvenient moments. Ogden instructed me to ferret them out, hold them up to the light and—where appropriate—consign them to the dust bin. He said, "Mac, get in there, clean out the engineers' drawers, I know they have a lot of stuff tucked away." So we launched an agency-wide review of pending projects, forcing people to either defend their brilliant ideas or wave them goodbye.

There was clearly a lot of stuff in the drawers, and arguably all of it needed doing, at least in the eyes of the people who made the plans. We were talking about wildly divergent work proposals—such as installing fiber cables in Korea and strengthening bunkers in the Seoul area for nuclear weapon communications systems in case the North Koreans invaded again. We also had many extensive projects underway in Europe such as a planned upgrade of the German telephone system (left over from Hitler's Third Reich) which I had learned about firsthand during my first German tour, and which we were using extensively. I would be using this knowledge a lot more in the years ahead.

More than once, I had to put on my smiling face and confront Colonel Coe telling him he was planning to spend too much money on projects that would not pay off downstream. My theme with him and others at Huachuca, and one I would repeat at all of my assignments over the years, was that our engineers had to learn to be more systematic about their plans. It was not just a matter of evaluating specific projects on their own merits. It was a matter of looking at overall systems, considering resources at our disposal and making decisions that made long term sense.

I made some enemies in those days, there was no way around it, but I tried to made amends as best I could. One such was an estimable fellow named John Grimes, a civilian employee of the Army who had served in the Air Force. In time, John and I became great friends and have remained so over the years. He later served in a number of prominent posts in Washington, including Assistant Secretary of Defense, and is today one of our nation's leading experts on cyber security.

I spent a good bit of time on the road, mainly back forth to the Pentagon in Washington on official Signal Corps business, but also seeking intelligence for my superiors who were always eager to know the latest inside information about who was in and who was out. One of my best contacts there was Colonel Bob Donohue who, like me, would eventually wear three stars.

We developed a good rapport. Spending some time in Washington, I came to learn Bob worked long hours until late in the evening. Back in Huachuca, I would call him every evening to get the latest, which I dutifully passed along to General Albright. We always wanted to know who was running the E Ring—the Pentagon floor where the big powers were.

I learned a lot during this first posting at Fort Huachuca about engineering big projects around the world, such as the worldwide command and control system infrastructure, built upon microwave systems, which were then state-of-the-art. A major challenge during the Cold War was assuring reliable, secure communications with our nuclear weapons facilities, especially those based in Europe and under the direct authority of the North Atlantic Treaty Organization (NATO). Any failure of communications in this area could have easily set off World War III.

Our nuclear deterrent capability was built on what we called the triad of airborne command posts that were more or less aloft at all hours of the day and night; the nuclear submarines called "boomers" that could launch nuclear warheads from just about anywhere; and the land based intercontinental ballistic missiles based in the U.S. and Europe. Any orders to launch nuclear missiles had to come from the President, and we had a variety of redundancies built in to make absolutely certain such an order was valid. Then as now, the threat of hackers to world peace is formidable.

It was all part of the Defense Communications System and the Army was responsible for all of the land-based communications system infrastructure. We had to answer for an incredible amount of circuitry around the world. We did not necessarily build it in the first place, but we were constantly rebuilding it to bring it up to date. We were responsible for the European Command and Control System (ECCS), a gaggle of microwave high frequency technology that connected our tactical nuclear weapons to the NATO headquarters in Belgium. On this first tour at Huachuca, I became intimately familiar with this system, how it worked, and how we maintained it and assured its security. I also became aware of potential vulnerabilities in the system, both to possible foreign sabotage or to system breakdown. It was and remains a heavy responsibility.

Another German Tour

After about a year in Huachuca-a busy year in which I learned a lot and got to spend some quality time with my family— I received orders to return to Germany for what would be my third posting there. The girls were in college so Barbara and I went off alone for the first time in a long while, empty nesters after all those years. Lynn and Marsha were living together, which we welcomed. We left them a little AMC Gremlin auto— remember those?—to get around in. We had few qualms about this arrangement; they were mature young women with good judgment who could take care of themselves.

I was first posted to the U.S. Army base in Mannheim as a brigade commander of the 22nd Signal Group, which later became 22nd Signal Command. We served the V Corps in the north of Germany and the VII Corps in the south. Everything strategic in the north became my domain, while another colonel was responsible for the south. The challenges we faced were different because of the topography. The northern reaches of Germany are relatively flat like Holland which makes the terrain amenable to radio transmission though you cannot reuse many of your frequencies because they travel too far. The rugged mountains of southern Germany make radio communication problematic. Even with high frequency radio, you can only transmit short distances with poor voice recognition. Even back in those days, everyone wanted good voice recognition. Given the technology of the time, we ended up relying mainly on wire down in that area.

Our biggest challenge and greatest responsibility was nuclear weaponry. We had a variety of communications networks that tied it all together, but we could take nothing for granted. There was the Soviet threat of course, but also threats of domestic terrorists—mainly the infamous Baader-Meinhof gang which, like some of the more radical groups back in the states, was communist oriented and inclined to violence. They assassinated military officers and blew up radio towers, causing us no end of anxiety and frustration. But it was the German government's problem; there was nothing we could do but be wary.

I had learned to speak a little German during my first two tours there, so I could order a beer or rent a room. I was travelling constantly because we had installations all over, not just in Germany, but also in England, Belgium and Italy. I had some capable people reporting to me, but never enough hands on deck. Most of my captains were very junior, so I requested a more senior officer to share some of my workload. They assigned to me an artillery major, soon to be a lieutenant colonel, who fit the bill perfectly.

The great concern that motivated us—beyond the prospect of a nuclear exchange—was that of a Soviet land invasion of Europe through the Fulda gap, the most obvious route for such an attack. Every year or two, the Army carried out Exercise REFORGER (for "return of forces to Germany) in which we moved armored divisions from the United States to Germany, or from the western part of Germany to the eastern part. I was responsible for communications on two of those exercises—one with the Big Red One and the other the Third Division. These were complex exercises, but we had it down to a science and knew what we were doing. Had the Soviets invaded, they would have had their hands full. A normal REFORGER exercise would take two to three weeks. Of course, in some cases we had to bring heavy equipment across on ships, which added to the duration. You really cannot move very many tanks by aircraft.

There had been some improvement in the quality of the troops in Germany since my previous posting, but not a lot. Many draftees were just filling out the remainder of their tours and had no interest in learning new technology. They preferred to raise hell—smoking marijuana, blowing off assignments and missing roll call. They knew that most of the time we would just try to move them along quicker rather than get bogged down in cumbersome disciplinary proceedings.

One of the pivotal introductions of computers onto the battlefield occurred during this period. My colleague and friend Colonel Alan Salisbury, was even then running the Operations Tactical data Systems at Fort Monmouth, and he and I were soon working together. "I brought over a handful of minicomputers—tactical computer systems—to the Third Infantry Division in Europe," Salisbury said. "He used them in REFORGER exercises. It functioned as both a computer and communications device. It allowed not just messages to be transmitted, but also graphics. Never before had all the echelons been able to have the same perception of what was going on in the battlefield." Salisbury returned to the U.S. as a brigadier general.

I had been in Mannheim for almost two years when I was asked to serve as Chief of Staff for General Dick Swenson, Commanding General of U.S. Army STRATCOM Europe. That promotion offered more responsibility, and also another move—this one to Worms, about an hour's drive from Mannheim, where STRATCOM headquarters was located. In that role, I was Swinson's alter ego, monitoring intelligence and operations staff. I was the key guy for strategic infrastructure. It was my job to keep all communications between the Army and the U.S. government operating smoothly, efficiently and securely. That level of responsibility is often a portal to higher command for an ambitious colonel like myself, but there were no guarantees.

This was 1975. The U.S. had withdrawn from Vietnam, but the stress of that difficult era was still very much in evidence. The Pentagon was reducing spending across the board and the military services were generally held in low esteem by the American public. I was busy with my work, but also having second thoughts about whether I wanted to spend my full adult career in the military—at least in that environment. I had acquired an extensive background in communications technology that was in ever greater demand in the private sector where West Point graduates have always been valued. For example, Jack Welch at General Electric and Harry Gray at United Technologies were aggressive in seeking out West Point graduates.

As if I didn't have enough to think about, Lynn got married that year in Las Cruces, New Mexico, in May, a week after she graduated from NMSU. Barbara and I came from Germany to attend. It was one of my happier duties—giving my daughters away in matrimony.

Back to Huachuca

In the summer of 1975, not long after Lynn's wedding, I got orders to return to Fort Huachuca. It was not completely clear to me why, but one never knows for certain in the Army why personnel decisions are made. You only know that somewhere in the Pentagon wise heads are planning your future, and you just have to assume they have your best interests, and those of the Army, at heart. In any event, we were happy to get back to Huachuca.

This time I was serving as Chief of Staff to Commanding General Jack Albright who, as head of Army Communications Command, spent a good bit of time back in Fort Monmouth and also in Washington. During his frequent absences, I functioned as base commander. Most of my counterparts in that role were brigadier generals or even major generals, but I was still a colonel and I was beginning to feel a bit put upon in that regard.

I got along well with Albright, despite the occasional reprimands for largely imaginary transgressions. He made a powerful case that the Signal Corps was too manpower intensive; that we should rely more on the private sector for many things. He never got his third star for some reason, possibly because few Signal Corps officers ever got to that level. In my book, he deserved one.

We were beginning to contend with the communications revolution in those days. The Army was becoming more computerized, but there was little sense among the computer people that it was not enough to accumulate tons of data if we lacked the bandwidth to transmit it, analyze it and use it effectively. We were collecting electronic data from all over the world, but did not have the manpower to handle it. As early as 1975, when I became chief of staff at Huachuca, I was involved in studies to merge communications with automation. This cause would occupy a good bit of my time and thought in the years ahead.

Albright retired in 1976 not long after I got there, and it fell to me to arrange and manage his retirement and the ascension of his successor, General Gerd "GG" Grombacher. Like Albright, Grombacher had a distinguished career, in part because like Albright he was not afraid to tell people higher up on the command chain that they were making mistakes. A German Jew, he had served with Army Intelligence during World War II as a prisoner of war interrogator, and later as an interpreter, winning a Silver Star. Grombacher played a key role building SAFEGUARD for the ICBM system when it came on line. He knew his stuff and was an excellent successor to Albright.

Anyone familiar with Army ways knows there is a complex protocol involved in retiring and promoting senior officers, and I invested a good bit of time in that event, but I got Albright into retirement and Grombacher into his office without a hitch.

So now I was Chief of Staff to Grombacher instead of Albright, but Chief of Staff nonetheless. Even so, my future in the Army did not look very promising to me at that time, in part because the Army did not look very promising. The military draft had ended in 1973 and we were building a volunteer force, but the volunteers we were getting in the 1970s were nothing to write home about. The Army was in disrepute in the post-Vietnam era. Parents simply did not want their children going into the military. We had to lure people in. There was a lot of corner cutting in terms of standards, and we ended up sorting out a lot of undesirables. In the Signal Corps especially we needed intelligent people. We provide education, but people who cannot read very well are unlikely to succeed in the Corps, no matter how much training they get. Also, the Pentagon was getting less funding as the services were downsized, meaning fewer opportunities for ambitious young colonels to move up.

I fell into some conversations with private sector companies about possible career opportunities that paid a lot better than the Army. Like many junior officers, I was tempted to make the jump. I had been in the Army for a bit more than a quarter century, and my career seemed to be stalled. So I updated my resume and on a whim asked General Grombacher to look it over. If I had been looking for reinforcement, perhaps subconsciously, I got it with interest. General Grombacher told me that I was highly valued in the Signal Corps, that I was needed, and— not incidentally—that a general's star lay in my future.

So I decided to stick it out, at least for a while. You might say I had stars—or at least one star—in my eyes.

CHAPTER 12

A Star Is Born

*Nearly all men can stand adversity, but if you want to test a
man's character, give him power.*
—Abraham Lincoln

I HAD BEEN A COLONEL P (PROMOTABLE) FOR A LONG TIME IN A
slot that was normally held by a brigadier general, sometimes a
major general, and I was getting a bit anxious about it, despite
the assurances from General Grombacher that I was on the list
for promotion. (Actually, Grombacher sat on the board that
selected generals, so he was in a position to know, but the key
question was when it would happen. I was not getting any
younger.) Finally, in 1977 I got orders to report to Fort Gordon,
Georgia, where at long last that star appeared on my collar. It
was a definitive moment in my career, a milestone in my sojourn
in the Army that had begun 25 years before when I was graduated from West Point. I had always had my eye on that star and
had worked diligently to earn it. It was most gratifying.

But I was careful not to get too full of myself. My mother had
given me some wise advice many years before, "Be careful what
you set your heart on, for it will surely be yours." In this case, I
accepted the promotion with pride, but without illusions. I had
by then become fully steeped in the vicissitudes of military life.
There is a certain amount of power that adheres to senior rank,
but it comes with a lot of responsibility, and you do not always

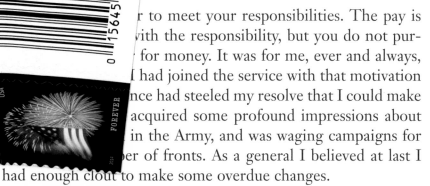

r to meet your responsibilities. The pay is
ith the responsibility, but you do not pur-
for money. It was for me, ever and always,
I had joined the service with that motivation
nce had steeled my resolve that I could make
acquired some profound impressions about
in the Army, and was waging campaigns for
er of fronts. As a general I believed at last I
had enough clout to make some overdue changes.

So Barbara and I were off to Fort Gordon, our first visit to
Georgia. Fort Gordon is a huge, sprawling complex on 54,000
acres about a three hour drive from Atlanta. Actually it is much
closer to Augusta, home of the Masters, and for a golfing enthu-
siast like me it was a wonderful place to be. There were many
excellent courses in the area, and you could play virtually year
round in that warm Georgia climate. Fort Gordon is the basic
training facility for Signal Corps personnel, but it also provides
training for regular infantry and a host of military specialties.
Counting all military and civilian personnel, there are about
30,000 people based at Fort Gordon at any given time. There is
always a lot going on there.

And as Deputy Commander, I was directly responsible for
much of it. The Commander was Major General William
Hilsman. Hilsman was not only smart, but he also had a lot of
energy. He brought into Fort Gordon courses in automated data
processing (ADP) that previously had been part of the Adjutant
General's responsibility at Fort Benjamin Harrison in Indiana.
Up until that time, almost all Signal Corps training at Fort
Gordon had been in communications. Hilsman also encouraged
the development of improved ADP software. The Signal Corps
was accustomed to software if you were dealing with encryption
codes, but the typical Signal Corps person was more attuned to
turning knobs and putting up equipment than in running com-

puters. The divide between communications and computing made less and less sense as the years wore on, which led to one of my more significant behind the scenes crusades.

To be sure, there was a merger of communications and computing already taking place in the machinery we worked with, but not in personnel skills. Even then the computer people were producing much more data than the communications pipeline could handle, but in those days there was no mechanism for dealing with that problem. Automation to a communicator meant getting rid of the old manual switchboards, with the operators working cords, and replacing them with automated switchboards that directed your calls. The Army was adapting slowly and awkwardly to evolving technologies in a desultory manner.

Part of this was due to a lack of leadership at the top. The office of the Chief Signal Officer had been abolished—foolishly in my opinion—back in 1964. That office was replaced by the Assistant Chief of Staff for Communications and Electronics. As ADP became more sophisticated, the title was changed to Assistant Chief of Staff for Automation, Communications and Electronics. But the Assistant Chief of Staff never did have the clout that the Chief Signal Officer once wielded.

The divide between automation and communications was for many part of a personal bias. Automation became a word despised by most communicators in part because it seemed to be taking over our world without rhyme or reason. Automation enabled Pentagon bureaucrats to send out tons of memoranda and reports to people all over the world at the drop of a hat. Everyone who has a computer today, which is just about everyone, knows what I'm talking about, but back then the technology was in its infancy. No one had a handle on it. There was something about the ability to send so much stuff out that fostered excessive communication. Officers all over the world were being deluged with information they had no use for, information that should never have been sent. I began a campaign to rein it in. I predictably encountered a lot of resistance, but quite a few fellow officers agreed with me and offered me their support.

But I had other things on my plate. One of my top priorities was to get the Signal Corps moving away from the traditional manpower intensive communications system based on wires. I managed to wrangle a temporary posting to Fort Monmouth in New Jersey where I led a panel of experts looking at new technologies available from industry in order to make recommendations for procurement. We needed to improve our capabilities and reduce the number of personnel required. That latter issue was critical because the Army was still struggling to attract quality personnel. We had a massive training operation underway at Fort Gordon preparing people for 52 distinct specialties. There are many narrow applications and it is hard to train people in the complexities of modern communications when they cannot read very well. We almost treated them like idiots—the red light comes on and you turn this screw, the yellow light comes on and you turn that one. I have always been a champion of the sergeants and warrant officers who always find a way to get things done in spite of their leadership, but I worried about the people we were taking through the system in those days. I thought we should be spending more time training fewer people in more depth. For example, the Navy spent 40 weeks training a technician, while we invested about a third of that time. But I could not change everything, at least not all at once. It would take us about 10 years, from 1975 to 1985, to build a professional Army, and in 1977 when I was first posted to Fort Gordon we were just getting started.

We were making significant progress in tactical communications. A major breakthrough already underway by the time I got to Fort Gordon was a new generation of combat radios called SINCGARS (Single Channel Ground and Airborne Radio

System). SINCGARS really did denote a major breakthrough for battlefield communications. The new radios, which handled both voice and data communications, are designed to be reliable, secure and easily maintained. SINCGARS uses 25 kHz channels in the VHF FM band from 30 to 87.975 MHz. It has single frequency and frequency hopping modes that hop 111 times a second. The SINCGARS family of radios-and it is a technology in constant transition—replaced the Vietnam War era synthesized single frequency radios (AN/PRC-77 and AN/VRC-12), although the two systems were interoperable. This was a recurring theme of my career in the Signal Corps—interoperability. When new technologies come online, there is always a long gap until the older equipment is fully replaced, especially with National Guard and Reserve Units. The SINCGARS were built to be mounted on vehicles, carried on backpacks, used in aircraft and even hand-held.

One would think that adopting the SINCGARS would be a no-brainer, but there is no such thing as a no-brainer in the military bureaucracy. We encountered resistance from some able people, not because they opposed the new technology, but because it was still evolving and getting better. One concern was the speed of encryption which is always a persistent problem with military communications. Some wanted to wait until it was perfect. I had long since decided that perfection is an elusive goal like the Holy Grail that we never quite attain. Our military units were saddled with obsolete communications equipment that needed to be replaced. We had the ability to give them something better now.

I won that debate, but not without a protracted fight with some of my best friends. It proved the right decision. The SINCGARS system has evolved over the years always getting better and better, and today more than 500,000 of them have been purchased and put into service.

Another innovation I backed during this period that proved successful was the mobile subscriber equipment (MSE), a multi-billion dollar investment that enabled the Army to acquire communications in remote locations where there is no cellular telephone capability. The MSE provides communications in an area of up to 15,000 square miles. The system is digital, secure, highly flexible and contains features that deal with link outages, traffic overload and rapid movement of users. A typical grid is made up of four to six centralized Node centers which make up the hub or backbone of the network. Throughout the maneuver area, ground troops and commanders connect to local call switching centers by radio or wire. These switches or extension nodes provide access to the network by connecting to the Node centers.

The MSE system provides both voice and data communications on an automatic basis using a technique called flood search routing. The system supports both mobile and wire subscribers with the means to exchange communications, data, and intelligence information in a dynamic tactical environment. The Tactical Packet Network (TPN) portion of MSE is a packet switching network that is overlaid on the circuit switching network of MSE. Along with providing data communications, the TPN provides data interoperability with adjacent systems, including commercial networks.

Today the MSE is deemed obsolete and is being phased out, which is the nature of communications technology. At the time it was a major improvement that increased our capabilities with fewer people. I was proud to be part of that.

Interestingly, one of the toughest little battles I fought during my first tour at Fort Gordon was to move a flagpole. I was responsible for both the Signal School and the Signal Training Center. When I got there, they had a flag flying over the Training Center instead of the Signal School which had the dominant role. I combined the commands of both and believed having the flag where it belonged would help convey that message, but there were serious people telling me I could not move that flagpole. I said, just watch me. We moved it.

Back to Germany

Just when I was up to my ears in a wide array of technical challenges, I got orders in 1978 sending me back to Germany for what would be my fourth and final tour. Barbara and I were back in Worms where I had three jobs: Commander of the Fifth Signal Command, staff Chief Executive for U.S. Army Europe, and Commander of the Worms Military District.

I was reporting directly to General George Blanchard, with whom I developed a warm rapport. But as fate would have it, within a few months I received my second star. Blanchard was nonplussed, to say the least. "Hey," he said, "you just got here, how did you get promoted so fast?" I explained that I had spent a great many years as a colonel doing jobs normally reserved for generals, and that at long last my record was catching up with me.

I was also working for Lt. Gen. Julius Becton, Jr., commander of the VII Corps in Southern Germany. Becton is something of a legend in the Army, the senior African-American general who even today, long after his retirement, exercises considerable influence on national defense matters. In fact, after he retired from active duty, he served as administrator of the Federal Emergency Management Agency (FEMA). On one occasion, President Reagan had him take over the District of Columbia Public Schools because they were in such sad shape back in the 1980s. When you have a tough job, Becton is the kind of guy you need.

Our primary concern in those days was the command and control of nuclear weapons that were very much on everyone's mind during the Cold War. There was the ever present danger that someone would compromise our communications system and send a false order to launch a nuclear strike. There were terrorist groups at large in Germany that would have been fully capable of such a thing. We knew our existing command structure, the European Command and Control Console System (ECCCS) was out of date and vulnerable. We replaced it with a state-of-the-art redundant system that was fully mobile. The Flaming Arrow Net was built on satellite technology and the other was a high frequency radio system called Regency Net. It was part of our SAFEGUARD system that any decision to authorize use of nuclear weapons had to be confirmed. We had to sell this new arrangement to many people who were quite understandably suspicious of anything related to nuclear weaponry, but we were persuasive and got it done. I slept a lot better after the new system was put in place; a lot of us did.

In my earlier tours in Germany, I had become familiar with the German telephone system left over from the Third Reich which was remarkably efficient. We learned to use it for our military exercises. Rather than lay wire along the roads and across bridges, with all of the disruption of civilian life that entailed, we tapped into junction boxes on nearby telephone poles. Of course we had to arrange this with responsible people with the German telephone system so they could free up circuits for us to use, but that was never a problem. It was truly remarkable how much that little innovation made our operations simpler.

We were still conducting the REFORGER Exercises in which U.S. based divisions were brought across the ocean and set up to engage an enemy force—-presumably the Soviets charging into Europe. By this time, REFORGER was old hat to me, and we relied extensively on our ability to use the German telephone system.

Also during this tour in Germany I assumed responsibility for modernizing the European Telephone System (ETS) which, though reliable, was still based on the old mechanical switching equipment and WWII era "cord board" operator assistance for long distance calls. We brought in state-of-the-art technology supplied by German companies. This had always been a critical element of my work in Germany-helping German companies acquire modern technology and develop their own capability. It was still the Cold War, Germany was still divided, and we were still nation building.

I was constantly on the move in Germany, and to other NATO nations, and I encountered a recurring problem that I would tackle later on. We had different and sometimes incompatible encryption systems. When I was aloft moving from one place to another, I would have to have at least two encryption code boxes with me as we passed from one sector into another that was using a different system. One did not need to be a genius to see how much trouble that could cause us were a war to break out.

As General Becton mentioned in his Foreword, I did in fact arrange for our troops in Germany to watch the Super Bowl. This was well before modern satellite technology made it possible to transmit signals virtually anywhere, and frankly looking back I cannot remember exactly how we did it, but I do remember watching the games.

And yes, I did score some points with General Becton when he asked me to merge several signal battalions into a centralized Signal Brigade, an abundantly obvious change of organization that was long overdue. I knew he had served in the all-black 93rd Division in WWII. So we branded it the 93rd Signal Brigade, a change that pleased General Becton immensely.

Behind the scenes, we were forever trying to fend off domestic pressures from fellow Americans who wanted to reduce U.S. forces in Europe, or get out of Europe altogether. As a senior officer on the scene, and one with extensive experience in

Germany, I understood the critical nature of the situation, the ever present peril of an invasion. In those days, the Soviet Union loomed as a major threat and communism was on the march all around the world. Germany was a critical breakwater in our national defense, an essential link in our commitment to provide for national security.

And I also found myself as the presiding general at a seemingly endless array of court martials, usually related to misbehavior of service personnel who should not have been in the service in the first place. We were still in the rebuilding mode for the Army, and we had a long way to go.

I had offices in Heidelburg and Worms, and moved back and forth quite a bit. Barbara and I were living in a tiny little house on the Worms military base that was not comfortable and certainly not appropriate for one with my authority. I went to the German government, I forget just who, and suggested that the U.S. commander deserved a better house. They readily agreed with me and built a new house.

Unfortunately, I never got to live in it but am told they still call it the "house that Mac built." After about two years in Germany, I got orders to return as Commanding General of Fort Gordon. It was not my first choice. I had fended off a possible assignment to NATO and lobbied for command of Fort Huachuca, but the Army had an important slot open at Fort Gordon and I was the most logical person to fill it. That's the way it goes in the Army. I saluted and reported for duty.

CHAPTER 13

Reformation

*Many attempts to communicate are nullified
by saying too much.*
—Robert Greenleaf
Essentials of Servant Leadership

MARK TWAIN WROTE ABOUT A MAN WHO HAD BEEN TARRED, feathered and run out of town on a rail. Asked how he enjoyed it, he said if it weren't for the honor of the thing, he would have just as soon done without it. I felt that way about being sent to run Fort Gordon in 1980. To be commander of a large Army installation like that is an honor, and is regarded as such, but it was still way down on my wish list. I wanted to go back to Fort Huachuca because I had serious ideas about what we needed to do to our communications framework, and Huachuca was where those decisions were being hashed out. But they needed a new commander at Fort Gordon and I was the most qualified candidate, so away I went.

At Fort Gordon, I was commander of the entire fort—not just communications. We had tens of thousands of people coming through for different kinds of military training. We were a critical part of the state economy, which meant I had a steady stream of state and local leaders coming to see me about this, that and the other. There was a lot that needed doing and I found myself wrestling with an intrinsic problem that most leaders have to deal with sooner or later, not enough resources to do what needs doing. I was doing my best while pursuing an appointment at Fort Huachuca, where I thought my talents were most needed.

This was in the waning days of the Carter Administration. The economy was a mess, what they called stagflation, with double digit inflation and double digit interest rates, plus long lines at gas stations that were forever running out of fuel. The Iranians had overthrown the Shah and taken employees of the American Embassy hostage. President Carter truly seemed in over his head and the Republicans had nominated Ronald Reagan who had a reputation, unjustly in my opinion, as a right wing kook. The Cold War was still on, and it seemed to many that the worldwide communist movement was gaining ground every year. But in the wake of Vietnam, there was no will to confront communism. The military was starved for resources and still trying to shake off the post-Vietnam blues.

In sum, I was under a lot of stress and, unbeknownst to me, it was taking a toll on my health. My health was not something that I worried a lot about. I had kicked the cigarette habit back in the mid-60s. Barbara fed me a healthy diet when she could, but I was constantly on the go and could not always get home for regular meals, or maintain a regular exercise routine. So it was that I was planning a trip to Europe in pursuit of some of my reform agenda when I had a visit from Lt. Gen. Richard G. Trefry, the Army's Inspector General.[11] I forget why he was at Fort Gordon, but as Army IG he was always visiting Army installations. He took a long, hard look at me, said I did not look well and urged me to see a doctor right away.

I took his advice and am glad I did. I went into the Dwight David Eisenhower Medical Center there at Fort Gordon. A

---

[11] Trefry, a good friend of many years, is another Distinguished Graduate of West Point.

stress test revealed the arteries serving my heart were blocked on both sides. One of the attending physicians said it was a wonder I was still breathing. They put me on a gurney then and there, administered strong doses of nitroglycerin and aspirin, and soon had me on an airplane flying to the Brook Army Medical Center at Fort Sam Houston near San Antonio, Texas, for surgery. When I got there, they had to put me aside for a couple of days because I had been taking so much aspirin to reduce the clotting ability of my blood. When the aspirin was sufficiently drained from my system, I received a quadruple bypass surgery. The operation took about five hours. They took a vein out of my left leg and spliced it in where it was needed.

Barbara and my senior enlisted aide got clearance to fly down and be with me while I was in post-op. Within a few hours they had me up walking around with hoses hanging from my body. I was weak and a bit disoriented, but determined not to stay in that hospital a minute longer than I had to. A few days later they let me fly back to Fort Gordon.

I was fortunate in having a deputy, Brigadier General Robert Donohue, and a chief of staff, Colonel Leo Childs, to cover my responsibilities while I recovered. Those guys were smart, reliable and dedicated.

"I was there when I was first a brigadier," said Donohue. "When Mac had his heart problem, I was left in command. I remember being told I had to testify before Congress on how much money the Army was spending on communications, and that I should not come within $1 billion of the actual amount. We had people all over the place doing things with little or no oversight. Every year we would use the year end money, like all government agencies do, to avoid having to return it to the Treasury and leave Congress thinking we did not need it. The Army had no real idea what we were actually spending."

Childs, another brilliant graduate of Northeastern University that has always supplied top notch Signal Corps officers, was one of my best people. "Mac was always focused on the quality of life for his troops," Childs said. "No matter how busy he was, the welfare of his troops was always foremost on his mind."

Of course, it takes a while to recover from heart bypass surgery, so I was off duty for a week and then on light duty for about six months before I was back up to speed. But I wasn't out of the woods yet. One day I took it upon myself to make a short speech to one of our signal companies and by the time I got home, I felt terrible. Barbara called an ambulance and they took me to the hospital. After a few tests, they determined that one of my bypasses was malfunctioning. They decided I was not in good enough shape to open me up again, but they managed to get me stabilized, and treated me with medication.

It was ruled a mild heart attack and I soon found myself before the Physical Evaluation Board. The Board quickly ruled that I was eligible for 100 percent disability, which meant I could have waltzed off into retirement with an ample income and spent my golden years playing golf and enjoying the sunset.

But I waived it. I wanted to stay on active duty. I really felt I had worked long and hard to get in a position to do some things that badly needed doing, mainly restoring the sense of unity the Signal Corps had lost when the Chief Signal Officer's post had been eliminated back in 1964. I had worked at every level of the Signal Corps all over the world and knew it backwards and forwards. Before I had the heart attack, it had been announced that I would take over at Fort Huachuca. I was determined to see that through.

Rightly or wrongly, I believed that there was no one else at that time in the Signal Corps with the credibility or the vision to achieve the systemic change that was needed to fully bring the Corps into the modern age. I wanted to finish the work I had started.

Return to Huachuca

In the summer of 1982, I at last got my wish—command of Fort Huachuca. I took over the Army Communications Command from my good friend who had encouraged me to stay in the Army years before, GG Grombacher. For the first few months, I was on a light work schedule because of my heart issue, but I gradually put that behind me and got back up to speed.

It was a good time for me and Barbara. The girls were out of college, married and living within driving distance. We had four grandchildren by then. They came to Fort Huachuca on a regular basis and we had ample room for them. The house we lived in on the base had been built in 1884. It had walls 18 inches thick, which made it virtually impervious to the weather, and a cupola up on top. I filled the cupola with books and spent what time I could reading and contemplating wonderful visions of making life better for people all around the world.

One day when Barbara was home alone a bear appeared out of nowhere and climbed up into a tree next to the house, making lots of noise. It proved to be an all-day event as military personnel tried to deal with the bear without doing it lasting harm. When I married Barbara, I promised to stand by her through thick and thin, good times and bad, but I didn't say anything about bears. They finally got the bear down and took it away to wherever they take bears. It did not come back.

Our personal fortunes were on the upswing, what with my survival of the heart problem, and being able to live where we wanted near our children, and the fortunes of the military were at last on an upward track. The new Reagan Administration was intent on rebuilding our national defense networks and reasserting our opposition to the communist challenge. It may seem strange to talk about it now, but back then it really did seem like our way of life—based on free enterprise and democratic values—was under siege and possibly in eclipse. The economic malaise of the 1970s, the expansion of communism into our own hemisphere, the rampant inflation and gas lines, and the hostage situation had combined to undermine our faith in who we are and what we stand for. An entire generation of intellectuals and commentators were telling us that capitalism was a dinosaur destined for extinction and socialism was the wave of the future. Now comes along this cheerful guy from California who is just bubbling with faith in the future of our country and determined to restore confidence in our traditional values. His critics mocked him and denigrated everything he said, but his gritty resilience shone through the haze of political rhetoric and awoke something in the American people.

It should also be said that Reagan benefitted greatly from at least one decision of his predecessor—the appointment of Paul Volcker to serve as head of the Federal Reserve. Volcker recognized the stifling impact of runaway inflation on our economy and used his power to set interest rates to bring it under control. The immediate result was a steep recession in which the economy did even worse and unemployment topped 10 percent. Everyone was calling for Volcker's scalp, and Reagan could have played politics at Volcker's expense, but instead he quietly backed the Fed chairman through an off-year election cycle that cost his party many votes. Hanging tough paid off. Within a couple of years, interest rates were down and the economy was growing again.

And the Army was getting the resources it needed to modernize—buying advanced equipment, attracting higher quality recruits and providing the training they needed to do their jobs well. We were not getting all we needed, not by a long shot, but after years of budget austerity, the infusion of resources came as a welcome relief. As senior communications officer, I had about

25,000 people under my command all over the world. We were not getting shot at in those days, but many of our people were still going in harm's way installing communications links in remote places that were hard to reach. People fell off mountains or were drowned. I had to write condolence letters to their spouses, a tough job that I insisted on doing personally. But they were my people.

I was constantly in airplanes and helicopters running around the world on official business, almost always to visit the troops in the field, though I spent a good bit of time going back and forth to Washington. I flew many hundreds of thousands of miles visiting our installations near and far. On longer journeys, say to Korea, I would fly commercial and then take a military plane to the facilities I would visit. I had air traffic control units in Germany, Hawaii, Korea, all over.

And of course, we had the usual run of personnel problems that always attend military service. Some enlisted man would start a fight in a bar. Some sergeant would get drunk and beat up his wife. Drugs were always around. I had to think—how can I make better policy to discourage that kind of behavior without becoming a dictator. I finally decided I had to beat up on my generals more, they could then beat up on the colonels, who would beat up on the majors and captains, and so on down the line. In the Army, if you care about your people, sometimes you have to beat up on them and send a message throughout the ranks.

At the same time, I was determined to evoke a more advanced way of thinking about the challenges we faced. I was working with people in the Army's Advanced Concepts Office. I told them we were expending too much energy to merely responding to requirements. We needed some creative people sitting off to the side taking a hard look, asking critical questions, thinking anew. Sometimes we in the military get too action oriented. I said, don't just do something, sit there. The hardest work we ever do, and the most important, is use our brains. Part of this process led to reducing our staff. We had way too many people stacking BBs.

I repeated a mantra I had employed from my first days in combat in Korea—give me more than one way to do something. In our business, you always need a backup plan, or two, or three. Most of our basic infrastructure in those days consisted of large microwave terminals dotting the landscape that cost an arm and a leg to build. It was expensive to build them and expensive to keep them operational. It could cost $30,000 just to paint one of those things, and they needed constant repainting. And of course any big storm could knock them down and put us out of commission. This was still in the early days of the communications revolution, but new technologies were coming on line all the time. I wanted to make certain our people were staying abreast of new developments, ever vigilant to find new, more reliable and less expensive ways to perform traditional jobs.

During a typical onsite tour of a communications relay facility, I would always ask, "Who changes the light bulb at the top of the tower?" It was usually one of the senior sergeants. I said why don't you train some of the junior people to do it? Because they are skittish about going up so high. I would never accept that. You're the commander. Get one up there.

A Signal Officer must be flexible. You have to be willing to get on a plane, fly around the world to remote outposts, and convince your people that you know what you are doing. That is what leadership is all about. Those were the kinds of duties I relished the most. There is nothing more satisfying to me than training people to do tough jobs.

The command posed challenges, but was not without its moments. One day my secretary said to me, "General Norstad is out here, he wants to see you." I was a student of history, and I recognized that name. Norstad was one of the youngest Air

Force generals of WWII, and later served as Supreme Allied Commander of Europe. So, in walks this ramrod straight tall gentleman who takes me by the hand and introduces himself. He was retired then and living in Tubac, Arizona, not far from Huachuca. He invited Barbara and me to his house for dinner, which I gladly accepted. Over dinner, I took the opportunity to gripe a bit about not having enough resources to meet the needs of the base and the Signal Corps. Norstad told me to relax, they would not have sent me out there if they did not have confidence in me and, by the way, I was going to get a third star. I told him I was glad to hear about the star, but that did not guarantee me more people.

Pivotal Events

I served as commander of Fort Huachuca, and the Army Communications Command, roughly from 1982 to 1984. During that time, we made progress on a variety of fronts, but there are three key things that stick out in my memory as pivotal moments in my career, and the future of the Signal Corps.

The first, and perhaps the most satisfying, was my promotion to Lieutenant General. Since elimination of the Chief Signal Officer's post, up until that time, I do not believe anyone in the Signal Corps had won a third star. It was a significant achievement and I believe one that reflected both my service and my vision of the future. I saw where the Corps needed to go, and I believe my superiors recognized that. It was a beautiful day out on the grounds of Fort Huachuca when the band played, the cannons were fired and that third star was pinned on my collar. I do not believe Barbara ever looked more beautiful, or more proud, than that day.

The second thing, and certainly one more significant to the Signal Corps, was the merger of our automated systems command with communications. I had fought for this many years and it did not come easily. Many senior officers in automated systems wanted their independence. They were leaning toward creating automation command, then under the adjutant general, and merging it with publications. But I told the higher ups repeatedly that was a surefire formula for protracted bureaucratic warfare. The computer people were running amok automating stuff right, left and sideways, and we simply did not have the bandwidth to haul it.

As a captain in Germany years before I had noted it took a long time to send data over a small circuit because we did not have broadband in those days. I was constantly at war with the ADP people who were forever overloading the system with more information than it could handle. Today we do have broadband and they are STILL overloading the system, only now it's a problem of more information than we can analyze.

I compare the situation to what we have with the Interstate Highway System today which is increasingly unable to handle all of the cars and trucks being poured into it. Gridlock is becoming commonplace from coast to coast, especially around major population centers. Infrastructure is always taken for granted, but it is very expensive to install, maintain and keep upgraded. And just as large trucks and SUVs tend to bog down traffic on major roadways, so do large data packages screw up electronic data flow through digital networks. There is only so much bandwidth, but left to their own devices and organizational imperatives, the computer people would continue producing ever more data ad infinitum. They insist on endless free rides over networks they do not understand and do not wish to help pay for.

One solution to this dilemma, of course, was to simply build more networks, lay more fiber optic cable, send up more satellites, do whatever was needed to carry more data. But it was becoming abundantly clear to me, and also to many others, that our real problem was getting a handle on the data being fed into the system. In my view, the communications people, who managed the networks, had to become actively engaged in sorting out what information was fed into the networks. To make that happen, we had to pull it all together under one tent.

I had begun working toward this at Fort Gordon and brought the idea with me when I came to Huachuca in 1982. Of course, no one ever achieves major shifts in military policy all alone. There were other senior officers who backed my approach, and at least one who was actively pushing the Corps in the same direction, my good friend Lt. Gen. Emmitt Paige, who was pressing for adoption of the emerging digital technologies into the system. Paige was at that time Commander of the Army Electronic R&D, and in an excellent position to help make this merger happen. Lest anyone think we were conspiring on this, I was really unaware of what he was doing, but as fate would have it, the two of us were on the same wave length. Our mutual friend and colleague, Lt. Gen. Julius Becton, looking down on all this from on high, says that Paige and I deserve equal credit for making it happen. I am more than happy to share that credit with Paige.

Thus was created the new Army Information Systems Command (ISC) based at Fort Huachuca that was commonly referred to as C3-command, control and communications. Later it was expanded to C4 when computers were added to the mix, and still later it became C5 when cyber security was folded into it. I was honored to serve as first Commander of the Army Information Systems Command, the modern equivalent of the Chief Signal Officer, until I got orders to report to Washington. When I left Huachuca in 1984, after only a few months leading the new consolidated command, I turned over command to Lt. Gen. Paige which was more than appropriate considering we two had done so much to make it happen.

The third pivotal event in 1983, and one that warrants mention, was the breakup of the Bell System, Ma Bell, as a result of an antitrust suit brought by the U.S. Department of Justice. Young people today may find this hard to believe, but up until then there was one and only one telephone system. If you wanted to call someone in the next house, city or state, you went through the Bell System. It was routine to dial "0" and summon an operator to assist you. Virtually all innovation in voice and data communications originated with Ma Bell at its laboratories in New Jersey. It was no accident that Fort Monmouth was near the Bell Laboratories that had been a fountain of communications innovation for more than half a century. Since time immemorial, the Signal Corps had enjoyed a close relationship with AT&T. It was one stop shopping and it was very effective. When war broke out, we would bring in hundreds or thousands of technicians from the Bell System who would serve until the crisis had passed. When we needed something new to solve a new communications problem, we worked with the Bell Labs. Even more often they came to us with new concepts they had developed.

The breakup of the Bell System has fueled an explosion of creativity in communications and cost competition that has served consumers well. But it made the military's jobs more difficult and challenging. We are not as reliant on the private sector as we used to be because the communications network is so diffuse. Much was gained by the breakup of Ma Bell, but some important things were lost as well. Those of us who came up through the old system still remember it with affection. Say what you will, it worked.

CHAPTER 14

Pentagon Years

*It's the only goddamn thing I've done in the Senate
that's worth a damn.*
—*Senator Barry Goldwater*

So Barbara and I packed up and moved to Washington, D.C., where over the next three years or so I would conclude my military career. It was my first permanent posting in the nation's capital, which makes me something of an anomaly in that I had earned my third star without ever doing time at the Pentagon. That in itself is highly unusual.

My new job was J-6 Director of Command, Control and Communications in the Office of the Joint Chiefs of Staff. That meant I was the highest ranking officer in the Signal Corps, the rough equivalent of Chief Signal Officer, a title that no longer existed. But whatever the title, I had made it to the top of the heap in my branch of the service, and was finally in a position to get some things done that needed doing.

We had a house at Fort Myer just across the street from the Officer's Club. Just around the corner lived a two star general named Norman Schwarzkopf, and a bit further away yet another two star named Colin Powell. I got to know them well and formed an opinion that they had great potential as leaders. Lynn and Marsha brought their families to visit us whenever they could. We were to enjoy many delightful visits from our grand-children. It was a good time.

Of course, my elevation meant that Barbara was now the "First Signal Lady," not that such a title actually exists, but she was expected to host social events for the spouses and friends of senior officers. Unfortunately, we did not have as much space in our Fort Myer quarters that we had in Huachuca. She ended up hosting teas under a big tent.

I was the third three star to hold the J-6 job, but the first one from the Signal Corps. My immediate predecessor had been an armored officer with a Ph.D. in nuclear physics who not surprisingly was focused on nuclear security. He insisted the Pentagon spend a pile of money hardening nuclear platforms to protect them from a high altitude burst of electronic magnetic pulse (EMP) that could easily kill all of our circuits, leaving us unable to respond to a nuclear attack. The brass did not want to spend the money, but I backed him up. I said it was life insurance and we had to have it to assure our readiness.

But I had a raft of more mundane but equally important issues on my agenda when I showed up in Arlington, the most basic being the ancient dilemma of allotting scarce resources among the military branches that were ever and always in competition with one another. Indeed, it often seemed as if the Army, Navy and Air Force were more hostile to each other than they were to potential enemies of the country. Despite a lot of talk about "jointness," active cooperation was more often the exception than the rule.

I spent much of my three years at the Pentagon trying to simplify command and control of the nation's nuclear defense system—the Triad consisting of land-based missiles, airborne missiles and submarine borne missiles. I perceived a gap between strategic and tactical systems and strove to fill that gap with a global system responsive to the President for whatever he needed. I sought a functional interface that worked. The evolving digital technology gave us powers we had not had before, but we were too slow seeing the potential and taking advantage of it.

I was an outspoken advocate that the Army should be intimately involved in all issues related to strategic communications simply because the Army was everywhere, with posts, camps and stations all over the Continental U.S. (CONUS), and around the world. We had to work closely with the other military branches; there were no two ways about it.

The ideal of course would have been one single, interoperable communications system for all of the services' tactical forces to use. In fact, we had made a stab at it years before with a system called Tri-Tac (Tri-Service Tactical C-cubed) but it quickly got out of hand. We developed a few things that worked well, but overall the cost structure was prohibitive and it became too expensive as a total system. There were in fact certain obvious differences among the services that mitigated against a single system, in addition to the traditional inter-service rivalry. For example, the Air Force and Navy operate from mobile platforms and can purchase entire communications systems carried in aircraft or on ships. The Army is tied to space (airlift and ship hauling capacity mainly) and geographic constraints. Thus, in general, the Army tends to buy C-cubed "piece-parts" that are relatively small, lightweight and easy for soldiers to operate and maintain in the field.

Within the Army, we had an unfortunate attitude of wanting to "move the garrison" to the field, putting a huge communications apparatus right next to the foxholes. We ended up with large, bulky, quasi-fixed, outsized equipment that was extremely difficult to airlift without more dedicated transports, which we were unlikely to have in a critical situation when every aircraft is needed. Each Army commander wanted his own computers and 32 clear channels. But you simply cannot take all that horsepower to the field without sacrificing communications capabilities. I spent a lot of time explaining that to people who did not want to hear it.

We had an even bigger problem related to the procurement process as communications technology was racing ahead, and new advances were appearing as fast as we could bring them online. Given the size of our military units and their dispersal all over the world, we faced a continuing headache with bringing online new equipment that was not interoperable with older stuff that was still in the system, and would be for years to come. This problem was particularly vexing with regard to the National Guard and Reserve units that are always at the end of the supply chain using yesterday's technology. Cost tradeoff decisions must be made constantly to avoid becoming too heavily capitalized in equipment which rapidly becomes obsolete.

All of which brought me to one of my chief concerns—system overload. We were even then wrestling with the challenge of connecting our 60-hertz (cycles per second frequency) minds to our megabit data pipes. We had become expert at moving mountains of data, but had not kept pace in terms of our ability to sift and sort critical bits of information to inform decision making. That was a critical concern in my drive to merge communications with data processing, but putting both under a single command in Fort Huachuca did not solve the problem. But it did, I hope, create a viable mechanism for dealing with the problem.

All of our challenges were greatly magnified by the divestiture of AT&T a couple of years before in which we lost our long-cherished one-stop shopping for communications technology and, in times of crisis, skilled communications personnel. As I stated before, it knocked the military for a loop. I had on my desk at the Pentagon a cartoon from a newspaper showing one worried-looking Soviet commissar talking to another: "Let's face it, comrade, any country that can break up the most efficient communications system in the world is not playing with a full deck."

All of a sudden, government agencies, the military and consumers were thrown into the wild and wooly marketplace looking for reliable providers of communications, and sources of communications equipment, with little guidance for deciding which was the most reliable and cost effective, and which companies were in for the long haul. In time, the breakup of Ma Bell would foster an incredible surge of creativity and innovation, but in those first years after the breakup we were strangers in a strange land. It was unnerving.

At the Pentagon, I served as chairman of the Military Communications Electronics Board (MCEB) that served to validate major communications systems and identify major funding problems before they were presented to the Joint Chiefs of Staff. I used that job as a clearinghouse for major technical issues, such as lack of interoperability and adequate funding. It was a constant challenge to weed out frivolous proposals that would entail vast expenditures without producing a bang for the buck.

But the biggest challenge of all, in my book, was people. We were going great guns with technology and equipment, but downplaying the human side of the equation. At a time when we really needed to bear down on more sophisticated training of communications personnel, we were increasingly giving it a pass. It was similar to the impact of technology on car repairs. In the old days, mechanics used to analyze problems and repair defective parts. Today they plug your engine into a computer and replace whatever parts are identified as the problem. They used to heat and beat damaged fenders into shape. Today they just replace them. A lot of people thought the Signal Corps should also operate that way.

I addressed some of my concerns in a speech to a meeting of the Armed Forces Communications and Electronics Association (AFCEA) in Fort Huachuca. "It's all well and good to say you only need to pull a card and replace it with a new one to fix it," I said. "I appreciate that no real training or understanding of how the part works is needed to repair a lot of automated equipment. However, my people may be a long way from the parts store during mobilization. Some of my people, in fact, are a long way from the parts store right now.

"We, as a nation, have focused on the flash and glitter of machinery and technology and we have sometimes relegated our people to a category along the same plane—if it breaks, get it fixed or, better yet, a new one," I continued. "But people are not disposable. They are not commodities. They don't have shelf lives or expiration dates. They have emotions, aspirations, and a never-quenched thirst for pride, esteem and a sense of belonging."

I left them with some sharp advice based on my three decades plus in the Signal Corps. "If the final product is to be data, learn something about automated data processing. If the final product is intelligence, learn something about intelligence gathering, sorting and application. If the final product is personnel information, learn something about personnel processing. I do not ask you to become an expert in those fields, just to find out what the customer wants to do with the information—notice I said 'information,' not 'data.'"

I conceded that robotics, artificial intelligence, lasers, photonics, etc. are important, but added that "none are more important than the man-machine interface research. Do not overlook the value of training in logic, reasoning, deduction and all the other drills which help people think better. Technology can assist in many ways, but in the foreseeable future it will be the *thinking person* who is the most important part of any system."

I often told my Signal Corps officers—you people are professionals. You are key members of the team, but you are not the quarterback, not even the wide receiver. You are the center. If you screw up, everything is screwed up.

Distant Thunder

I was having a good old time running amok among the brass hats working to improve the military communications networks and capabilities, focusing attention on serious challenges we needed to deal with, and I felt I was really getting somewhere.

But life has a way of interrupting our best laid plans and sending us off in unexpected and unforeseen directions. So it was that I would spend most of my time at the Pentagon as senior communication officer, not working with communications challenges, but helping the military services cope with their first massive reorganization since 1958.

Over the preceding years, there had been several incidents putting a spotlight on serious problems in the military chain of command—namely the continuing inability or refusal of the main branches of the military to work together effectively. There was a lot of talk about "jointness," but for many if not most officers serving in joint commands, the first loyalty was to their branch of service.

The lack of cohesion created breaks in the chain of command that led to disasters. In April of 1980, during the waning days of the Carter Administration, U.S. forces attempted to rescue the American hostages held in Iran (taken from the U.S. embassy in Teheran when the Shah was overthrown). The operation, called Eagle Claw, was cancelled by its commander following a catastrophic helicopter-airplane collision in the desert that left eight American servicemen dead. A critical defect of the operation was the ad hoc nature of the mission's planning in which soldiers selected to participate were picked, not according to their capability or training, but to be sure all four services (Air Force, Navy, Army and Marine Corps) were included so they could all share in the glory. We ended up with Marine pilots flying Army commandos in Air Force helicopters off Navy ships.

There was a catastrophic breakdown. There was no glory to be shared.

In 1982, the Chairman of the Joint Chiefs of Staff (JCS), David C. Jones, initiated discussion of JCS reform in testimony before Congress, and also an article in a military magazine. His theme was that structural inadequacies of the system were responsible for bungled missions, not the quality of individuals involved. The fundamental flaw was that the chiefs had dual and often conflicting loyalties to their respective services and to the JCS, and the chairman himself lacked authority to force consensus. As such, he was unable to fulfill his primary mission of providing military advice to civilian decision makers. General Edward "Shy" Meyer, the Army Chief of Staff, lent his voice to that of Jones. While Jones and Meyer offered competing solutions, they agreed the existing system was inadequate.

A year later, on October 23, 1983, as if to underscore the problem, two Shiite terrorists driving a bomb-laden truck destroyed the Marine barracks at the airport in Lebanon killing 241 military personnel in what proved to be the worst single day disaster for the Marines. In the aftermath, bitter inter-service rivalry paralyzed the Joint Chiefs of Staff that was unable to come up with a retaliatory plan. While they bickered, injured Marines were being flown back and forth all over Europe while the services fought over which would be allowed to treat them. It was a miracle none of them died in transit.

Two days after that, U.S. forces were sent into Grenada, an island in the Caribbean, to oust a Marxist government that was trying to create another Cuba. Once again, the primary purpose was not to achieve the military objective but rather get all of the services in action. The Marines took the northern part of the islands while the Army went into the southern end. Special operations were carried out by both the Army's Delta Force and the Navy's SEAL teams. As the Pentagon's senior communications officer, I saw many of my warnings about the need for interoperability of communications underscored. Army units were unable to communicate with Navy vessels to guide offshore supporting gunfire. Army officers even flew to the Navy command ship to coordinate and another Army officer used a Marine radio on the ship to call other Navy ships, but was unable to because he lacked the Navy codes to authenticate his requests. In fact, no Navy representatives attended Army planning sessions, and no Army representative or Air Force forward controllers (who deployed with land forces in order to coordinate close air support), were present when Navy aviators received their missions. Since each service bought its own communications equipment independent of each other, there was little interoperability.[12]

In sum, it was a classic Chinese fire drill of miscommunication and sometimes total lack of communication that could have spelled disaster had we been up against a more formidable foe. It was becoming increasingly clear to people in and out of government, including the Pentagon, that the existing military chain of command was in dire need of repair.

The impetus for reform got support from yet another source, the President's Blue Ribbon Commission on Defense Management, generally referred to at the Packard Commission because it was chaired by David Packard, one of the founders of Hewlett-Packard. The Reagan Administration was orchestrating a massive military buildup in those days, and there were many stories in the news media of conspicuous waste and inefficiency. One of the things I have learned through my years in the service is that it is a terribly difficult thing to spend a billion dollars and get your money's worth. There were several specific items that resonated with the public—a $435 hammer, a $600

---

[12] There were reports in the news media of soldiers on the ground making calls on local pay telephones because they had no other way of connecting with their commanders.

toilet seat and a $7,600 coffee pot. President Reagan charged the Packard group to review "the budget process, the procurement system, legislative oversight and the organizational and operational arrangements, both formal and informal, among the Office of the Secretary of Defense, the Organization of the Joint Chiefs of Staff, the Unified and Specified Command Systems, the Military Departments, and Congress."

In its report submitted to President Reagan on June 30, 1986, the Packard Commission recommended, among other things, that the Chairman of the Joint Chiefs of Staff become the primary military advisor to the President, that the Joint Staff report to the Chairman and that a Vice Chairman substitute for the Chairman in his absence. In a word, it recommended a clear chain of command, a not unfamiliar concept to the military establishment.

A second and possibly even more important endorsement of reform came from the Center for Strategic and International Studies (CSIS), a highly-regarded Washington think tank (with which I have had a long association). The CSIS report analyzed the full spectrum of defense issues from joint operations to budgetary planning to weapons acquisition. The CSIS report recommended sweeping changes throughout the defense establishment, and included a foreword endorsing its recommendations from six previous Secretaries of Defense.

But there were many powerful opponents of reform. Secretary of Defense, Caspar Weinberger, was adamantly opposed to reform, arguing that public scrutiny of the JCS's inadequacy reflected poorly on the military and threatened the Reagan Administration's buildup. He may also have feared that a stronger Chairman of the Joint Chiefs would threaten his control over defense policy.

The Navy also was nearly apoplectic in opposition to reform. Secretary of the Navy John Lehman and several admirals testified against it. Indeed, there were elements in all of the services opposed to reform because having a centralized military authority to filter the services budgetary requests, and to evaluate the services policies, would reduce their ability to compete for more resources in the chaotic political process, which they were quite good at. It would be hard for the Navy or Marines to insist they needed more funding if the Chairman of the Joint Chiefs had already recommended reducing that service's budget.

Momentum was building for major reform led by Senator Barry Goldwater (R-AZ), Chairman of the Senate Armed Services Committee, and Rep. William Flynt Nichols (D-AL). Senator Sam Nunn (D-GA) also played a leading role. There were many at the Pentagon who supported reform and many who opposed it, but all were skittish about trying to influence the outcome lest they seem self-serving. It would be an understatement to say that the Pentagon was scared by the reform initiative because there was no way to predict how it would turn out and whose ox would be gored. I was actively engaged in the negotiations in part because I had a relationship of sorts with Senator Goldwater stemming from my command at Fort Huachuca which was in his state. I do not mean to imply we were close friends, we were not, but we did have a rapport. We had many conversations about the need for reform and what it should entail.

It seemed like every time I turned around, I was talking to either the Packard people or the Goldwater people. Shy Meyer was by then retired, but he also was fully engaged in the debate. He and I made the same points over and over—-at we were spending way too much building systems for the different services that did not work together. I may have talked too much, but given the diversity of opinion at the Pentagon, there was no one to review or direct my input.

Goldwater was taking a lot of heat, but he was serving out his final term in the Senate and in any case was not averse to heat. He was a crusty old guy, a retired Air Force officer who knew the military in and out. He was also a ham radio operator and respected my area of expertise. We both were acutely aware that the Pentagon was a cumbersome bureaucracy in which the right hand often had no idea what the left hand was doing. I recall on one occasion, probably in exasperation, telling him he could walk the floors of the Pentagon and dismiss every other person without damaging national security. He knew I was joking (I think).

The four-year effort begun by Generals Jones and Meyer resulted in the Goldwater-Nichols Department of Defense Reorganization Act of 1986. It sought to achieve eight specific objectives: reorganizing DOD and strengthening civilian authority; improving military advice given to civilian decision makers; placing "clear responsibility" on the commander in chiefs (CINCs) for accomplishing missions of their commands; ensuring that the CINCs authority over their forces was commensurate with their responsibilities as CINCs; increasing attention to strategy and contingency planning; encouraging the more efficient use of defense resources; improving joint officer management policies; and enhancing the effectiveness of both military operations and DOD management.

The law did not specifically address communications, but the clear focus on joint decision making and management set the stage for a sea change in the way we operated. As fate would have it, I had only a few more months of service after the law became effective, and the changes were still rippling through the Pentagon bureaucracy as I decamped.

So it happened to me twice—I set the stage for a unified command of communications and automation in Fort Huachuca and was quickly moved on to Washington, and I helped usher in a new era of military management, and quickly moved on into retirement. In both cases, I had to pass the baton to others to build on the structure I had helped put in place for them.

But Goldwater-Nichols achieved most of its desired objectives, and was fully on display in the 1991 Gulf War (Operation Desert Storm) where it functioned exactly as planned, allowing my former neighbors, Chairman of the JCS Colin Powell and General Norman Schwarzkopf, to exercise full control over Marine Corps, Army, Air Force and Navy assets without having to negotiate with the individual services. The result was an overwhelming victory.

And a key part of that victory, shown nightly on network TV news, was the central control headquarters where ranks of officers huddled over laptop computers before a giant video screen closely managed the complex movement of a massive military operation covering thousands of square miles of land and sea. That was real time communications in action. I do not believe any military had ever gone to war with a more closely synchronized operation that was made possible by an incredible communications network. I watched that drama unfold with pride, knowing I had made a major contribution.

CHAPTER 15

Booz Allen Hamilton

Never fear the want of business. A man who qualifies
himself well for his calling, never fails of employment.
—Thomas Jefferson

I WAS USHERED INTO RETIREMENT IN 1987 BECAUSE THAT WAS
the regular schedule for senior Army officers. I had served in the
Army 35 years and had no prospect of reaching higher rank. It
did not reflect poorly on my service, but rather is the established
convention of the Army. After a certain point, you must move up
or out. I was a bit disappointed in that I had aspired for a fourth
star. I believed I was a viable candidate for the southern command because of my extensive experience in Latin and South
America, but it was not to be. Those postings generally go to
senior officers of the infantry or armor. I had taken a career in
the Signal Corps about as high as it could go. At least no one
before me had risen higher.[13]

But I was still a young man with a lot of good years left, and
there was an abundance of opportunities out there for me to take
advantage of my experience and still make contributions, in both
the military and civilian worlds. As retirement loomed, I was

---

[13] In February 2012, it was announced that Lt. Gen. Dennis L. Via of the
Signal Corps has been nominated for promotion which will make him the
first four star general from the Signal Corps.

talking to several different organizations that expressed an interest in me, and even had my name being bandied about as a possible head of the National Security Agency (NSA). That would have been interesting given my career-long battle to restrain NSA's obsession with encrypting everything. In fact, that may have been what killed the idea.

At one point, I had tentatively agreed to become president of the Armed Forces Communications and Electronics Association (AFCEA), a private sector association representing a broad swath of people in my field. But then Booz Allen Hamilton came to me with an offer I could not refuse.

I knew them well. Booz Allen is one of the oldest and most distinguished management consulting firms. The firm was founded in Chicago by Edwin G. Booz with the theory that companies would be more successful if they could call on someone outside their own organizations for expert, impartial advice. In 1940, the company was hired by the Navy to help lay the groundwork for World War II. Since then it has built an impressive reputation providing management advice to both government and private industry. It has been deeply involved in some pivotal developments such as the breakup of Ma Bell, the organization of the National Football League, and modernizing the Internal Revenue Service. (The latter item could possibly use a bit more work.)

Booz Allen has always had a major focus on helping business and government use technology wisely and effectively, which was why they wanted me. I was to work with them on information technology management for 11 years, during what was to prove a period of intense growth for the company. When I went to work there in July 1987, they were generating about $500 million a year. Today, Booz Allen, headquartered in the Washington, D.C. area, has about 26,400 employees worldwide and generates annual revenues of more than $5 billion.

Moving from the Army into the private sector was a bit of a culture shock for me. I had not worked in the private sector since I was a boy saving money for college. I had grown accustomed to the perks of being a general, having people salute when you walk into the room. During my final posting in Fort Huachuca, I had commanded 30,000 people around the world. Even at the Pentagon, I had a staff of 170. At Booz Allen, I had a secretary.

Booz Allen, then as now, had a reputation for exemplary integrity. They were focused on earning profits of course, but were exceedingly careful to make sure they did it honorably. The Booz Allen code of ethics was taken seriously throughout the organization, and I appreciated that. As a senior Army officer, I was well aware that not all government contractors were quite so fastidious about their conduct.

The Booz Allen people told me they wanted no partners older than 55, but said they might make an exception for me. They compromised by making me a Senior Principal, whatever that is. I really did not care about the title; I just wanted a job.

I was given an open-ended assignment to help Booz Allen develop business. My superiors were not too particular about what kind of business it was, as long as it was profitable and, of course, honorable. Some of Booz Allen's business was with government and part was purely commercial. The commercial side of the business was run mostly from New York City, Paris, Rome and other international capitals.

But I was assigned to the unit working on information technology for the government which was my field. This work was centered mostly in major U.S. cities located near major military clients, such as San Diego, Boston, and, of course, Washington, D.C. As a rule, the contracts we had with government were of longer duration than in the private sector. There was always a friendly rivalry between the government and commercial sides of Booz Allen. In fact, I believe it was a bit more than that. The commercial people tended to look down their noses at the people working on technology and information issues, and the people on the tech side definitely made less money.

Government contracts were at least one year, often longer, with provisions for extension. The commercial business usually brought contracts lasting 30, 60, 90 or maybe 120 days. On the commercial side, Booz Allen usually worked with senior management of Fortune 500 companies. On the government side, we tended to work with senior and middle management which is where effective agency decisions are made. The top people are generally political appointees who spend most of their time charming the White House and Congress.

My experience was in communications with a focus on large scale systems. My challenge was to find a way to leverage my background with some of Booz Allen's clients, in particular their military clients where I was well known and my experience was appreciated. It helped that I still had all of my security clearances and would keep them until I retired from Booz Allen in 1999. Today, of course, more than a million people have security clearances. It has become something of an insider's joke in Washington where they are routinely handed out to people who have no need for them and, in more than a few cases, should not have them.

One of my first projects was to work with the Electronics Industry of America (EIA) helping the organization forecast what electronic requirements would be five or 10 years down the road. Of course, this was in the late 1980s leading into the 1990s when communications technology was just beginning to take off on a dizzying ride of unprecedented progress still underway today. Even so, the work was right down my alley. We were working with systems I knew inside and out, and I doubt if there was anyone out there better qualified to analyze where all this was leading.

I became intimately involved with EIA and other professional associations that were working to help government agencies refine assessment of their IT needs in order to seek funding from Congress. There was a lot of money involved, and the bureaucrats were reasonably concerned that they make sound long-term decisions, lest they end up with expensive but obsolete information systems. In the modern world, obsolescence can come quickly with digital technology.

"Mac did excellent work pushing Booz Allen into work with professional communities," said Marie Lerch, Booz Allen Vice President for Marketing and Global Relations. "Also, the whole jointness thing, that Mac brought with him from his work on Goldwater Nichols, was new to Booz Allen. He not only helped us adapt to the new era of jointness among our clients, but also helped us learn how jointness applied to us. We had divisions that did not talk to each other. Mac helped us deal with that."

"Mac wasn't just fascinated with the potential for technology to enhance international security and education," said Ralph Shrader, Chairman and Chief Executive Officer of Booz Allen. "He did something to make it happen-through his client work with the C4I community, his pioneering role in distance learning, and his professional leadership in AFCEA and other organizations."

Advanced digital communications is a complex field that demands extensive integration. Booz Allen was not then known for its ability to integrate systems. The real integrators were the aircraft producers like Boeing, Lockheed Martin and Douglas that were involved in integrating demands of fleets and airports.[14]

Booz Allen was normally a subcontractor working within some of the large defense contracts for major combat systems. We were noted for our ability to work with government agen-

[14] Martin Marietta was still separate from Lockheed at the time.

cies helping them interface pieces of the IT puzzle. There was a lot of merging and acquisition among defense contractors during that uncertain period, so we were always on our toes.

During my early years with Booz Allen, I was working extensively with defense contractors so my expertise in the finer points of the Goldwater-Nichols Act, which focused extensively on military procurement, stood me in good stead. In fact, I put together a book for the AFCEA describing in minute detail revisions in the acquisition policy then underway. Then as always, I looked at the big picture helping our clients develop effective large-scale systems within the new defense procurement environment. This project enabled me to work with both senior and junior people at Booz Allen early in my career with the firm, which enabled me to gain their confidence, settle in and become an effective part of the team.

I did encounter a few glitches along the way. Over the years, I had developed a habit of reaching out to people both above and beneath me in the pecking order to help them contend with the challenges of rapidly evolving communications technology. Offering friendly advice had become second nature to me, but it was not appropriate within the Booz Allen scheme of things. "Mac," one of the senior partners said to me one day, "you must understand that we do not give this information away, we sell it."

What a concept! One interesting thing I did learn from this—most people tend to attach more value to your advice when you make them pay for it. Makes sense, I guess. Anything that is free tends to suggest it has little value.

They also—and this was really scary—made me learn how to use a personal computer. Up until then, I was a victim of a fairly common CEO affliction—having the power to delegate things like that to subordinates. I treated computers like fancy typewriters and I, as a three star general, did not type. But Booz Allen rescued me from that mentality, for which I will be always grateful. I got online and never got off, albeit in a hunt and peck mode.

Math and Science

By 1992, I was working with the Defense Advanced Research Projects Agency (DARPA) that had been created in 1958 to help make sure the U.S. maintained its technological leadership over the Soviet Union during the Cold War.[15] DARPA employs some of the smartest people in the nation working on projects that have great impact on our future. It was DARPA that invented the Internet, initially as a means for academic researchers to share information. Naturally, those super bright people don't tend to stay with DARPA for very long because the private sector always beckons with more lucrative opportunities, but they are invariably replaced by even smarter people.

I had come to know several people at DARPA when I was on active duty at Fort Gordon and Fort Huachuca, mainly working with them on innovative concepts for packet and digital radios. But even then I was developing a keen interest in educational programs for our nation's youth, particularly in math and science. There was as yet no concept of STEM (Science, Technology, Engineering and Mathematics) in those days; that would come later. But years of working with woefully unprepared enlisted personnel in the Signal Corps had given me a sense that our public schools were doing a poor job of educating the next generation.[16]

My concern about education dates back at least to my first tour of duty at Fort Gordon when I came as a colonel P (promotable) serving as deputy post commander, and soon acquired

---

15 DARPA was ARPA and then DARPA again. I could never keep up with the name changes.

16 "A Nation At Risk," the famous report deploring the poor performance of public schools, had been published in 1983.

my first star. After I was there four months, we got a new commander, Major General Bill Hilsman who, as I mentioned elsewhere, was surely one of the most intelligent people in an Army uniform that I ever met. Hilsman was on the road most of the time leaving me to run both the Signal Corps training school and the post, which meant I had more than enough on my plate. But one of Hilsman's better ideas was construction of a National Science Center for youngsters. He recognized a need to expose more of our nation's young people to exciting things going on with modern digital technology in a time when most public schools were still oblivious to it. He thought we could sell it initially as an expansion of a small museum we had there housing a few artifacts from Signal Corps history, but that was a modest affair. Hilsman wanted something grand. He suggested we initially call it the U.S. Army Signal Corps Communications and Electronics Museum as a noncontroversial way to get it started-which we did-but it quickly morphed into the National Science Center.

I thought it was a worthy idea, though I did not have much time for this project. Still, Hilsman was the boss so I tried to do what he wanted. Soon I found myself in trouble for using government money to make a film about the National Science Center, but that and other promotional efforts had an effect. We put on displays for local school children who were bused in to visit. We always had helicopters on the floor for them to crawl around on. Anytime we could get something from NASA it was a big draw.

I somehow managed to get this project into the recruiting budget, and soon we had two big 18-wheel trucks—we called them "Mobile Discovery Centers"—hauling around our science and technology displays to schools near and far. The purpose was to teach young people that studying science and math is fun, as well as essential to their future. Each unit included a mobile theater seating 30-35 and showing programs about math, science, electronics and computers; a mobile classroom providing training for students and teachers; and a mobile, walkthrough exhibit hall showcasing small interactive exhibits and displays.

"Mac was a proponent of the National Science Center, as was Hilsman," said Lt. General Robert Donahue who served as my deputy when I commanded Fort Gordon. "They worked the local gentry in Augusta for support. One of the locals owned a shopping center that they used as a base when they put together an organization, both military and civilian. This was in the early days of the digital revolution when most school kids were not getting exposed to technology in class. It was mostly a general education for kids. We also used it as a recruiting tool, though we did not advertise it as such."

We went so far as to develop extensive plans for construction of the National Science Center in Augusta, but for a variety of reasons, it never got built. To this day, I harbor hope of building a home for the National Science Center on the mall in Washington, D.C., where hundreds of thousands of youngsters troop through every year visiting national landmarks and museums. It would be a natural fit and do a world of good.

Online Learning

My work with the National Science Center whetted my appetite to do something for the nation's young people if only because I believed they were being bypassed by the digital revolution. I don't mean all of them of course. There have been legions of bright young people in the forefront of the digital transformation all along, and not a few of them have made great fortunes from it.

But the vast majority of our young people were stuck in the same old public schools doing the same old routines at the beck and call of teachers who were also trapped in a time warp, oblivious to the changing world around them. I believed we were missing a great opportunity to use the new technologies to improve the public schools—not least by bringing the technology into the schools and training the teachers to work with it.

At the time I was working with DARPA on some project, I forget just what, but my DARPA contact was an exceedingly bright fellow named Mike Kelly who shares my background in electrical engineering, had a sterling career at IBM, and has taught at least three first rank universities over the years. As it happened, Mike was crusading to get a computer on the desk of every K-12 student in the country, an ambitious proposal that many people thought was both desirable and doable.

It must be remembered that in those days Japan was running circles around us in technology and our government was increasingly concerned about our loss of leadership. In 1987, Congress created SEMATECH (Semiconductor Manufacturing TECHnology), a government-sponsored consortium of 14 leading U.S. semiconductor manufacturers to enable them to pool resources and knowledge to compete more effectively against the Japanese. DARPA was the conduit through which Congress provided $500 million to SEMATECH. Kelly played a key role in that operation. Kelly was driven by a genuine, lifelong concern about the quality of education in this country. The semiconductor manufacturers, of course, were motivated by the prospects of profits. But the notion of computers on every desk was part of the SEMATECH vision.

The plot thickened. Mike put me in contact with a real life tech entrepreneur named Jack Taub, now deceased, who had helped launch one of the first online networks, The Source, which he later sold for a substantial amount of money. Jack shared our expansive vision of how digital technologies could be used to transform K-12 schools. Jack in turn was working with a young vice president of the U.S. Chamber of Commerce named Jeffrey Joseph who also saw the power of technology to transform public schools. The U.S. Chamber of Commerce was very concerned about the quality of public education in our country, reflecting growing anxiety among business leaders that our nation's young people would not be able to function in the workplace of the future.

"I have been consistent in trying to get technology into the classroom," Kelly said. "The most important element is the teacher. Today, one third of all teachers come from the lower third of their graduating class. This has to change. I compared this with what they are doing in Finland where only graduates in the top tenth are accepted into teaching. The most important aspect of improving education needs to be preparing teachers to use the technology."

"There is a growing body of evidence from research, schools and workplaces in a variety of settings around the country that sophisticated communications technologies offer the promise of quantum advances in education and learning through more individualized instruction," Joseph told the House Committee on Economic and Educational Opportunities in 1995. "In part, this is simply because modern students and workers are much more acclimated to using advanced technology than earlier generations were, and commensurately less receptive to the old, pedagogical teaching technique."

Joseph spelled out the promise of using digital technology to empower teachers. "Properly used, the high tech classroom can accommodate all students at their individual speeds and needs," he said. "Thus, teachers will no longer be required to seek out a middle ground of progress, leaving slow students behind and boring brighter ones. By merging interactive technologies with other teaching techniques, instructors can accommodate each student's abilities and interests."

Before long, I was working with Kelly, Taub, Joseph and others in pursuit of ways to transform this vision into reality. Not surprisingly, given my background in the military, we were able to interest DARPA (then in its ARPA phase) in our vision. The result was the Community and Learning Information Network (CLIN) which was envisioned as a catalyst to enable community groups to come together within the context of private sector networks. Our original vision was that the private sector would provide the basic information tools and technologies for the new system and once that plan was operational, CLIN would be dissolved.

In reality, we found it slow going generating interest among educators. Public school systems then and now are highly resistant to reform suggestions from outside academia, or even from inside academia for that matter. The public school infrastructure in our country is like a huge ocean liner that will take a long time to turn around—presuming we can ever persuade the captains that it needs turning. Business leaders were more receptive to the vision, especially Booz Allen, which saw the potential market.

In 1992, Booz Allen, in alliance with 18 other corporations, 16 state governments, the U.S. Chamber of Commerce and DARPA launched CLIN as a joint initiative to enable a "culture of competence" across the nation creating an infrastructure that would be available. We were soon operating out of offices on K Street, and seemed to be on a roll. The Clinton Administration, with Vice President Al Gore leading the way, was definitely interested in the CLIN vision. We asked DARPA for $90 million to get CLIN fully mobilized, and were told we might get $30 million, which would have got us off the ground.

Then politics got in the way, as it often does in Washington. The U.S. Chamber of Commerce had been in negotiations with the White House about health care reform, but when Congress took it up, the Chamber reversed course and went all out to

BOOZ ALLEN HAMILTON   195

defeat it. The Chamber's legislative efforts, as always, were led by the same Jeffrey Joseph who was working with CLIN. As soon as the White House identified this connection, the DARPA money disappeared.

The National Guard

Undaunted, Joseph bypassed the White House and went to Capitol Hill in search of political support. He found it with Senator Robert Byrd (D-WVA), the wily Mountain State legislator who was ever and always on the lookout for creative ways to channel federal money to his constituents. Senator Byrd inserted a $7.5 million earmark for a regional distance learning project that would see a pilot program in West Virginia.

The focal point of this distance learning project was the National Guard. The National Guard, the oldest military institution in the U.S., was challenged by its responsibility to maintain a combat ready military and emergency force with diminishing resources. Through Senator Byrd's office, we offered the CLIN vision as a practical solution to its dilemma. Using the technology we had developed, the Guard—and later the Army Reserves as well—could provide onsite interactive training in local communities where its members lived, saving a lot of money by not having to move people around the country.

No sooner did we get the language in appropriations legislation than we had a visit from a high ranking officer from the National Guard who was adamantly opposed to the project. He said the Guard would refuse to work with us and would tell Congress to keep the money. I was never sure whether this intervention was ordained by the White House or if it was just another case of the old Washington "not invented here" syndrome. In any event, I made a few calls to the Pentagon and Jeff made a few calls to Capitol Hill, and we eventually persuaded the Guard to take the money and launch a distance learning system.

Of course, the Pentagon had to put its own label on the program which became the Distributive Training Technology Project (DTTP). The original $7.5 million earmark funded demonstration sites in West Virginia, Virginia, Maryland and Pennsylvania. It proved popular and successful and grew by leaps and bounds. By 2002, we had $300 million invested in 310 training sites in all 50 states plus four territories.

These high tech communication centers have proven their value time and again. For example in the wake of 9/11, as rescuers rushed to assess the devastation in Manhattan, New York Army National Guard officials used the DTTP classroom capabilities to create a point-to-point audiovisual link with state emergency officials to help assess the status of gas lines, electricity and telephone connections. Guard command staffs in New York, New Jersey and Connecticut used the DTTP's continuous video teleconference capabilities to conduct briefings and coordinate their rescue efforts for everything from troop deployments to providing meals.

Today, the DTTP is the world's largest distance learning network enabling the Army National Guard to meet its education requirements by linking 3,200 armories and supporting multimedia computer training for 362,000 citizen soldiers. The Army National Guard has deployed more than 200 distance learning classrooms nationwide. In addition to armories, the classrooms are located in local schools, libraries and community centers to ensure that access to these resources is available to the broader civilian population. The centers are run on a fee-for-service basis so that states can rent network access to federal agencies and the private sector on the 28 days a month when the Guard is not using them.

This system was to my knowledge the very first online interactive learning system of any type and we had visions of greatness. We (CLIN) aspired to use these National Guard/Reserve centers as prototypes for the nation's public schools, showing the world how online learning could transform the educational process. It was and is an exciting vision with great promise.[17]

But we ran into some unforeseen hurdles that conspired against our vision, or at least have delayed its realization. The first and most obvious is a wall of indifference in the educational establishment that is actively hostile to outside input, especially from sources not traditionally seen as part of that establishment. There was also widespread ignorance of and resistance to digital technologies that is still conspicuous among educators.[18]

The second hurdle was a rush of private for-profit companies using online technologies to market education and training, many of which we believe were and are using proprietary technology that we developed. Widespread abuse of this system, much of it funded by government education loans, has sparked public concern and review by Congress. Our vision had always been for using technology to promote learning on a not-for-profit basis, but the for-profit sector had more resources and beat us to the punch, at least in terms of some important target audiences.

Last but not least was a decision by former Defense Secretary Donald Rumsfeld to finance the war against Iraq on the cheap by pillaging the National Guard's resources, including the funding needed for the DTTP. This is a topic that is much bigger than its impact on the DTTP, and beyond the purview of this book.

---

17 In developing this online technology, CLIN won approval of several patents that in our view embrace just about everything being done today in terms of online education and training. The matter is currently before the courts.

18 *The New York Times* of January 4, 2012, carried a front page story about teachers in Idaho refusing to adapt to computer technology as required by a new state law.

I still see a great potential for a National Science Center in Washington, D.C., and the use of CLIN technology to enhance the quality of K-12 education. I hope I live long enough to see these things happen.

Bowing Out

Toward the end of my time with Booz Allen, I had opportunities to work with foreign dignitaries who were interested in the changes going on in digital communications. For example, we helped Thailand develop a better surveillance system along their borders. Working with foreign envoys requires finesse and social graces that I had acquired during my various postings overseas, and of course Barbara, as always, was a sophisticated hostess.

Epilogue

A man by himself is in poor company.
—Eric Hoffer

I RECALL A LOW POINT EARLY IN MY MILITARY CAREER WHEN I really considered packing it all in. I had just returned to the U.S. from India where I had been keenly depressed by the abject poverty of the vast majority of people, as well as the offensive caste system. Back home President Kennedy had been assassinated, which was disconcerting for all of us, and we were raising the stakes in Vietnam. The country was entering a period of social unrest, uncertainty and self-doubt. I had been posted to Fort Riley where I found myself out in the bitter Kansas winter struggling to manage the load-out of the Big Red One as it prepared to move to Southeast Asia. And I was living in some dismal enlisted men's quarters where I could not hang my fatigues in the closet because it stank and the bath had no shower, which left me smelling pretty ripe anyway. It was not a happy situation.

But I soon shook off the blues and got lost in my work because I enjoyed the people around me, and it was clear they needed me. From the first day of my service in the Signal Corps, I have loved the people I was privileged to work with up and down the line. The Army is a social organization. Everything you do is as part of team. As you rise through the ranks, the intensity of your relationships is magnified. You are not only working with a diverse group of people, but you carry increasing responsibility for their welfare, success and happiness, in addition to the important missions you are assigned to.

Over the years, I have counseled many young officers and enlisted men, and I have advised more than a few of them to get out of the service at the first opportunity, not because they lacked intelligence or ability, but because they lacked the essential capacity for human interaction that I believe is essential in the military. I am thinking of one fellow in particular, a young officer, who came to me frequently to criticize his colleagues, always complaining about one thing or another. I told him he was a self-generating genius, which he was, but that he should get out of the service. He simply could not work with other people. He ended up in the private sector working as a very successful architect.

That young man grew frustrated when he was compelled to do things he did not want to do. We all have to wrestle with that to some degree, and perhaps it is more common in the military environment where you are rarely asked whether you want to do something. It is a fact of life that time flies when you are doing what you want to do and drags when you are doing tedious, unrewarding work. But being compelled to perform rote tasks has a way of clearing your mind and empowering you with discipline to achieve greater things-if you come to it with a positive attitude.

Some people are drawn to the military because they believe the command structure will give them discipline and help them compensate for their lack of people skills. But while the command structure and rigid discipline of the Army can help people acquire discipline, it also puts a premium on people skills, even more than the private sector. At every hour of the day and night in the military you are intensely engaged with other people. You may or may not like them as individuals, but that is neither here nor there. You depend on them and they depend on you. If you do not genuinely care about other people, if you cannot find satisfaction in helping other people succeed, a military career is not for you.

Leading people is the greatest and most rewarding challenge a person can ever have. A true leader gets people to do things they do not want to do because they trust his judgment and know he will not ask them to do what he would not do himself. General (later President) Dwight D. Eisenhower used a piece of string lying on a table to demonstrate his concept of leadership. He would invite someone to push the string, which of course is impossible. But then he would pull the string and get immediate results. It is that way with people, he said. You do not push them, you pull them. And to do that in the military, of course, you have to be out in front of them.

In 2002, I returned to West Point for the 50th reunion of my graduating class. A group of us prepared some talking points on leadership that we published in a little brochure for the cadets who were about to be graduated. I contributed a few items. First and foremost, I advised the young officers to be very careful who they married because a military spouse, be it a woman or a man, will have to make many sacrifices to support your military career. I have had more than one good friend tell me that I would never have made it to the upper echelons of the Army without my life mate Barbara who always kept me on an even keel, possessed in abundance the social graces that I lacked, and had my back over a lifetime. I suppose this is good advice for anyone, but it is especially vital to any military officer who aspires to rise through the ranks.

I advised them also that when people under their command are injured or sick, you move heaven and earth to get to that hospital or sickroom and offer whatever encouragement, sympathy and assistance you can. The old adage of officers eating last is as valid as ever. You make sure your people have food, water and dry clothes before you worry about your own comfort. You take care of your troops; they will take care of you.

When young officers ask me how I made general, I attribute

it to driving in everyone else's lane. I encourage them to broad-
en their perspectives beyond their assigned specialties and gain
a higher perspective on what is going on, always looking for the
big picture. You have to do your job of course, but you will never
get anywhere in the military by staying in your lane.

Any military officer needs a sense of humor, preferably of the
self-deprecating variety. We do not need more strutting mar-
tinets. So much of what we do is tough no- nonsense discipline
that it can undermine morale and make enlisted people resent
you. A good hearty laugh will cover a lot of sins and make your
people want to work for you.

And I will suggest also that another critical element of rising
through the ranks—and one that may well seem counterintu-
itive—is an ability and willingness to speak truth to power at
inopportune times. I am aware that this is inherently risky. "I
insist that my people always tell me the truth," said the movie
mogul Samuel Goldwyn, "even if it costs them their jobs."
People at the top of the pecking order, whether in the military
or private sector, do not relish criticism. But every young man or
woman on the way up will sooner or later encounter an order or
project that is poorly conceived and destined to fail, sometimes
with calamitous results. When this happens, if you are an Army
officer, you are obliged to do what you can to save the Army, and
maybe the country, from calamity.

The good news is that you can almost always find people in
the chain of command who will respond to legitimate concerns
and intervene where necessary. First, of course, you must make
absolutely certain that you are right. When I was a young lieutenant at Fort Monmouth trying to conduct training without use
of the appropriate equipment, it was clear to me where my
responsibility lay. I filed my reports as required and refused to
stop filing my reports when confronted by a superior officer.
Granted, this was not a big thing, but it raised eyebrows. Even

so, someone above me in the pecking order must have recognized I was doing the right thing. It obviously did not derail my career.

When I was a young major helping move The Big Red One from one place to another, getting it ready to deploy to Vietnam, I did not hesitate to tell senior commanders they had to change their schemes for their maneuvers. I would say you can't do that because you will have your division rear in front of your major command post and be unable to move it. You must move your communications equipment back further. They listened to me and did as I said because they realized I was right.

It is another matter entirely when a senior commander like General William Westmoreland insists on pursuing a disastrous military plan as he did in Vietnam in what proved to be the greatest U.S. military calamity of my lifetime. It is neither reasonable nor practical for junior officers to get engaged in policy debates at that level. But there were people at the White House and the Pentagon who should have reined Westmoreland in. They failed to do their duty, and the country suffered immeasurably for it. I have always been willing to speak truth to power when I believed it was called for. But I always made sure I was right, and because I was right, I have gotten away with it.

I greatly admired President Ronald W. Reagan and believe he deserves great credit for restoring our nation's confidence in its values and commitment to the future, after a long period of national soul-searching. But when called upon by senior government officials to evaluate President Reagan's infamous Strategic Defense Initiative (SDI) that called for a high tech missile apparatus to shoot down incoming nuclear missiles, I shared my skepticism with all who would listen, including some highly placed military and government leaders. I do not believe I was being disloyal by pointing out that the technology of that era would not support such an ambitious scheme, and that in any event there was not enough money in the world to fund it. I had spent much of my career interconnecting with air defenses and in my book air defense was always a loser. It costs four or five times as much to build a defensive system as it does an offensive system.

At some level, I believe SDI was never meant to be taken seriously, but rather was part of a public relations campaign to pull the rug out from under the Soviet Union. If that was the plan, it was successful. The communists could not keep up with the Reagan Administration's military buildup, and the Soviet Union disintegrated.

The moral of the story, I suppose, is that sometimes even foolish ideas, or at least ideas that seem foolish, can have positive results. It is well that we have convictions and are willing to take a stand for them, but a certain amount of humility always serves us well. I have been wrong many times. No one of us has all the answers. I have made many mistakes over my career, but was always willing to listen to criticism and to respond to it. Beware the leader who walks on water. First and foremost, don't be that leader.

Accomplishments

As I look back over 35 years of military service, plus 25 years and counting beyond that, I ask myself a hard question: did I make a difference? Did I push the ball forward? Did I really accomplish anything worth crowing about?

I am a poor country boy who has seen a lot of the world. I have done very well in the Signal Corps, becoming the first Army Signal Officer in some 20 years to be promoted within the Army to three stars. I learned a lot about leadership at West Point, and even more amid the hustle and bustle of real life. I learned a lot about large scale systems at the University of

Michigan. I learned a lot about humility and friendship at the War College. I have decoded many mysteries of electronics and space, and have shared my insights with senior leadership. It was a heady experience to work closely with great patriots like Secretary of State George Schultz, Secretary of Defense Caspar Weinberger, Senator Barry Goldwater and Senator Sam Nunn. And of course, I have known and worked with many of the great military leaders of our times. Were I to begin naming them all, I would quickly run out of ink.

I have reached my sunset years still nurturing a love-hate relationship with the Signal Corps. I have spent my life serving the needs of our nation in peace and war. I love the people—the officers and troops—without reservation. But I unequivocally hate the greed and poor judgment that motivates certain elements of the military-industrial complex to focus on technology without calculating the cost and impact on our country. A stark example that sticks out in my memory was the great uproar about the supposed Y2K calamity that was anticipated when computers came in contact with the new century. It never happened. Many of us were skeptical about it, but the greedy people hyped it all out of proportion to persuade the government to spend billions on automated data processing equipment that was not needed. It was money down a rat hole, money that should have been spent for other things. I have seen this happen time and time again.[19]

Today the boogieman of communications is the so-called cyber war which has legions of self-proclaimed security experts raising fears and looking for opportunities to sell Uncle Sam yet more billions of equipment that we do not need and cannot afford. There is no question that the world harbors many bad actors who are constantly striving to compromise national secu-

---

[19] Within the military, Y2K was actually handled very professionally under the leadership of a "czar", Lt. Gen. Peter Kind, former G-6 of the Army, who is now retired.

rity secrets, and even more who are trying to steal proprietary information from U.S. companies. Every large U.S. company, and most of the smaller ones, must spend substantial sums protecting their secrets from digital pirates. But there is not nor can there ever be a definitive security system that will totally assure security, any more than there can be absolute security for bank vaults. There is an endless war of attrition between the pirates and those with confidential information, and as in every war we will always have victories and defeats. The question we must always address—the one I have wrestled with for most of my career—is how much security is enough, and how much security can we afford. We all must live with the possibility of being robbed or mugged, but that does not mean each one of us should have a security guard walking alongside of us when we go to the grocery store. There is a limit to how much security we need, and what we can afford.

I have lived through a revolution in communications technology and seen many wondrous advances since the days I was laying communications wire along the ground in Korea and keeping carrier pigeons handy in case the wires did not work. I am fully aware of the remarkable capabilities of the new digital technologies—and am even more acutely aware of their limitations. We have gone from carrier pigeons to tweets—and I frankly believe the tweets—those 140 word messages of banality—will soon join the pigeons among the more curious artifacts of history. I have yet to encounter or hear tell of a memorable or significant "tweet." Almost all tweets are just noise. No significant thought can be expressed in 140 words. We are all—civilians and military alike—awash in more information than we want or can assimilate. Gradually people reading tweets will realize they are wasting time and that they should be reading more important things.

This is the fundamental conundrum posed by modern communications technology—its capacity to inundate us with more data than we can handle or know what to do with. It is a critical challenge that runs throughout government. The security agencies in particular seem enraptured by their ability to capture voice and electronic messages from all over the globe that are largely packed away in storage for lack of capacity to analyze it. Too late we discover that we had advance notice of terrorist activities afoot, but the information was never analyzed and used.

It is a basic tenet of mine that we must sift through mounds of data to identify a few precious bits of knowledge here and there, and then must assay that knowledge in great detail in order to derive a few random bits of wisdom. Wresting wisdom from the mountains of data is a tedious, time-consuming process that demands critical judgment. It demands people who think, not tweet.

Over the last 20 or so years of my military service, and continuing into the present, I have waged a low-wattage battle against the proliferation of information, often useless and irrelevant, that is overwhelming both our ability to transmit and comprehend. Some of my colleagues have ducked this fight entirely, insisting our job is only to transmit the information and let others worry about where it comes from, what it's about and what to do with it. But I believe we have a greater responsibility than that. When the problem was too little information, we strove to fill the gaps. Today our challenge is to stifle the excessive flow, to restrict it to a manageable level. Permitting too much information into the system is unnecessary, excessively costly and counter- productive because we lack the capacity to analyze it efficiently.

The problem of information overload is compounded by the widespread compulsion to encrypt everything we send, regardless of its sensitivity. Encryption is a very cumbersome, expensive process and offers no guarantees. Certainly anything up on the web is vulnerable. The Internet cannot be totally protected because it is multi-noded and offers so many entry points. You can make people work extra hard to break your code, but they will always find a way.

Our obsession with security and safety has long since passed the point of diminishing returns. We now spend upwards of $300,000 to protect a battle worthy Humvee from a $5 improvised explosive device.

When I was at the Pentagon during the Reagan Administration, Secretary Weinberger had a most capable Assistant Secretary of Defense named Don Latham who permitted me to raise objections to many items in the communications and intelligence budgets. I would like to believe I helped identify and kill many bad ideas. But in terms of the greater problem—the endless avalanche of mostly useless information—I was a voice in the wilderness. Many agreed with me about the problem, but we were all at a loss what to do about it. In the end, it depends on thousands of people at key points in the system raising their hands and saying "Enough!"

I never wanted to build a watch, I just wanted to find out what time it was. Many good people in the Signal Corps have squandered their careers because they became overly focused on technology. Technology is a tool, nothing more, and cannot solve every problem.

"High technology is a resource that thrives in the U.S., but our country is struggling to maintain its high technology leverage in world markets," I said in an article in *Signal* magazine in 1988, as prescient an observation as I ever made. "Command, control, communications and intelligence (C3I) systems that employ high technology can be the force multiplier and catalyst for producing a more stable world if properly developed and deployed. Software and hardware lone cannot solve the problem—C3I systems must be created for people, and people must be constantly in the center of the calculus of creating, developing, testing and deploying them."

And the challenges of transmitting tactical information on the battlefield remain with us despite all of the massive breakthroughs of the digital age. As I write, the Army is lamenting the expenditure of $6 billion on a new program called the Joint Tactical Radio System (JTRS or "jitters" in Army parlance) that was to replace nearly all older radios in the U.S. arsenal with "universal" radios, thus simplifying communications and freeing combat units to "tap into the network on the move," in the words of an Army spokesman.

The result is soldiers tramping through Afghanistan burdened with different kinds of radios sprouting a forest of plastic and metal cubes sprouting antennae of various lengths and sizes, including short range models for talking with nearby units, longer range versions for reaching headquarters 25 miles away, and a backup satellite radio in case the mountains blocked the transmission. Those mountains in Afghanistan are even steeper than the ones I had to deal with in Korea. My heart goes out to the troops trying to tote those loads up those Afghan hills. It brings back cold memories and is yet another case of grand ambition colliding with the unbending laws of physics. After years the Army is relearning what we experts have been saying for a long time-it is impossible for a single radio design to handle all of the military's diverse communications tasks. Technology is wonderful, but it cannot solve every problem.

Come to think of it, we may have been premature in abolishing the pigeon program.

Thinking and Believing

I am a slow learner, and God has given me additional time to try to unravel the mysteries of life. My strong faith in God has pulled me onto the "high road" of decision making. My own personal grief throughout my lifetime has tempered my feelings for families that suffer with dysfunctional members that cause problems for both family members and others. The book of Ecclesiastes (citing Solomon) reserves true wisdom for God alone, and suggests that man should obey God's commandments, and all will be well.

Most Americans seem to take their freedoms for granted. That is human nature. But as a military man, I am keenly aware of the cost of those freedoms, from the blood of the first patriots who purchased it for us, to that of our young people today who continue to pay the price. Our freedoms are dearly bought.

I have little patience for those Americans who fret about immigration. We have always been a nation of immigrants. Every generation brings more immigrants to our shores seeking to participate in the American dream. God help us if we ever close the door to them.

The greatest threat to our way of life is not terrorism, but ignorance, poverty (often caused by lack of family structure), and corruption. Our foreign enemies can do us harm, but cannot bring us down. Only we can do that.

The real joy of living comes not from wealth or possessions, or even knowledge and understanding, but from helping others and serving mankind. There is no space for vanity in a successful person's makeup.

Golf

Over the past six decades, my love of golf has been a tremendous source of physical and mental wellness. Recovering from open heart surgery was hastened by my strong desire to return to the links. Golf is an individual sport that can be played with a group or alone. It can be a character builder because it demands shrewd judgment and control of your emotions. The relationships you begin on a golf course can extend across a lifetime. The ability to speak truth to power, a talent I have taken to extremes, can be cultivated on a golf course. I have also found that playing golf with foreign leaders can help reduce cultural barriers. I really do believe that if world leaders would embrace golf, and use it as a means to communicate with other leaders, there would be fewer global conflicts.

My good friend Gen. Frederick "Fritz" Kroesen believes, and I agree, that you can learn an awful lot about a man's character on a golf course.[20] A fellow who loses his temper and acts badly on a golf course is unlikely to do well leading soldiers. To truly love golf, as I do, you must be at peace with yourself, and able to accept your own shortcomings. Because I don't care who you are, Mac McKnight or Tiger Woods, sooner or later, golf will humble you.

One of my favorite memories was playing the famed Masters Course in Augusta, Georgia. That was a dream come true for me, as it would be for any true golfer. I was retired from the Army by then, but discovered that my love of golf would be a terrific asset in the business development world. I do believe that both business and diplomacy can be more easily pursued on the golf course than in a sterile conference room. And after 10 long years of war in Iraq and Afghanistan, I am hopeful that some of our wounded warriors will be given an opportunity to take up golf as an outlet for their troubled souls.

Critical Thinking

After all is said and done, our marvelous technology cannot supersede the need for critical thinking by people endowed with

---

[20] Kroesen contends, and I agree, that a senior officer who does not play golf should never be put in command of a military base that has a golf course. Invariably, he will stint on the funding to keep the course in proper shape.

good educations and practical experience to weigh the information and make informed decisions. Technology is a wonderful tool, but only a tool. The most important link in any complex system is the human being with ability to think critically, question authority and seek to do what is right.

And all of the technology in the world is no substitute for the faith and values that sustain us through our darkest hours and enable us to triumph over adversity. I have never critiqued anyone's religious faith and I never will, but you had better believe in something. I do believe there is a greater power than all of our technologies and weapons, and we need to open our eyes, minds and hearts to it.

At the end of the day, success is not measured by power on the ground or money in the bank. We measure it, each one of us, by what we see in the mirror. If you are content with that image that looks back at you, then your life is a success. If not, you have work to do.

Our country will never have complete defense or impenetrable cyber security or totally reliable communications. There will always be breakdowns and confusion. Today as in 1953 when I went to war in Korea, the ultimate communications challenge is to always have a backup plan. There is no certainty in war or peace, and never can be. Our only timeless assets, as Saint Paul said so long ago, are faith, hope and love—and the greatest of these is love.

Index